Frederic William Macdonald

The Latin Hymns in the Wesleyan Hymn Book

Studies in Hymnology

Frederic William Macdonald

The Latin Hymns in the Wesleyan Hymn Book
Studies in Hymnology

ISBN/EAN: 9783744768139

Printed in Europe, USA, Canada, Australia, Japan

Cover: Foto ©Thomas Meinert / pixelio.de

More available books at **www.hansebooks.com**

THE LATIN HYMNS

IN THE

WESLEYAN HYMN BOOK

Studies in Hymnology.

BY

FREDERIC W. MACDONALD.

London:
CHARLES H. KELLY, 2, CASTLE STREET, CITY ROAD, E.C.
AND 26, PATERNOSTER ROW, E.C.
1899.

CONTENTS.

CHAP.		PAGE
I.—Historic Survey		1
II.—The "Te Deum"		12
III.—Veni, Creator Spiritus		25
IV.—Veni, Sancte Spiritus		40
V.—Charlemagne and King Robert of France		53
VI.—Cantemus Cuncti Melodum		59
VII.—Jesu, Dulcis Memoria		69
VIII.—Hic Breve Vivitur		82
IX.—Hora Novissima (*continued*)		94
X.—Veni, Veni, Emmanuel		107
XI.—Supreme Quales Arbiter		115
XII.—Jam Lucis Orto Sidere		127
XIII.—Angularis Fundamentum Lapis Christus Missus Est		135
XIV.—Dies Iræ, Dies Illa		146

THE LATIN HYMNS
IN THE
WESLEYAN HYMN BOOK.

CHAPTER I.
Historic Survey.

IN the Hymn Book published by John Wesley in 1779, which, with a few hymns subsequently added, continued in common use among "the people called Methodists" till 1830, there are, as might be expected, no hymns from the Latin. The time for this had not yet come. The treasures of Latin hymnody were practically unknown, and many things must happen before either English Churchmen or Nonconformists would care to explore them. It was in a different direction, as is well known, that Wesley turned in search of hymns that might be sung in the Societies under his care along with those of his brother Charles, of Watts, and of Doddridge.

HISTORIC SURVEY.

His early association with the Moravians had made him acquainted with the hymn-writers who represented the most spiritual element in the Protestantism of Germany during the latter part of the seventeenth and the first half of the eighteenth century, and from these he translated a considerable number of hymns with great skill and success. They possess, indeed, the highest merit to which translation can attain. They are as living and as effective in their new as in their original form. They passed into the spiritual life of Methodism as readily, and with as gracious a power, as the hymns of Charles Wesley himself, and they keep their place to the present day among the most cherished hymns of Methodism the world over. Of this the reader may assure himself by calling to mind Zinzendorf's "Jesu, Thy blood and righteousness"; Gerhardt's "Jesu, Thy boundless love to me"; Tersteegen's "Thou hidden love of God, whose height"; and Rothe's "Now I have found the ground wherein," with many others. These are more than felicitous translations in a literary sense.

They are translations in which not only the form, but the spirit, the unction, the vitality are carried over from one language to another without loss or enfeeblement.

This German element in the Hymn Book of English Methodism was not only valuable in itself, but as furnishing links of kinship with Christians of other lands and other Churches, and witnessing to that family life of Christendom which is bounded by no seas, and stretches across the dividing lines of language and of race.

In addition to twenty more hymns from the German, Wesley included in his Collection of 1779 a translation from the French of Madame Bourignon, and another from an unknown Spanish source; but it contains nothing from the Latin, nothing from early Christian or pre-Reformation sources, although as early as 1747 a metrical version of the *Te Deum* by Charles Wesley had appeared in *Hymns for those that seek and those that have redemption*.

The *Supplement* to Wesley's Hymn Book, consisting of 209 hymns, was issued in 1831.

In this *Supplement* the first notes of Latin Christian song are heard. Charles Wesley's paraphrase of the *Te Deum* and a translation of the *Veni, Creator Spiritus*, "Creator Spirit, by whose aid," were the only hymns from the Latin in use in Methodist congregations until the publication of the enlarged hymn book of 1876. This may seem to be but a slender and timid borrowing from so rich a treasury, but it could hardly be otherwise. No movement had as yet set in towards the study of Latin hymnology either from a historical or a devotional point of view. All interest in the subject had been practically dead for more than two centuries.

This is somewhat noteworthy when the facts of the case are considered. The Reformers and the first generation of Protestants were by no means disposed to leave the best hymns of Western Christendom an undisputed possession of the Church of Rome. Luther and Melancthon had been brought up on the hymns of the Breviary and the Missal, and never abandoned their use; and they loved to sing them in their original Latin. Further,

Luther translated many of the principal ones into German, including the *Veni, Creator Spiritus*, *O lux beata Trinitas*, and *Veni Redemptor Gentium*. Continuity of pre-existing religious faith and devotional life—corruptions and abuses cleared away—was the great Reformer's aim, and not a new beginning in everything. He did not think it needful to add to the shock he was compelled to give to the accepted order of things by discouraging the use of hymns well established in the sentiments and traditions of the people. To those who knew Latin he commended the hymns as they stood, and for those who did not he prepared German versions of them. And in this he was followed by the divines and scholars of the next generation, and indeed by German hymn-writers for a century or more, so that, directly and indirectly, the influence of Latin hymnody in the Lutheran Church was deep and lasting.

In the period that followed the Council of Trent there was, indeed, a rivalry, conscious or unconscious, between Roman Catholic and

Protestant scholars in collecting and editing the old Latin hymns. The *Elucidatorium* of Clichtoveus, published in 1515, a noble monument of learning and zeal, until lately quite indispensable, and still of the highest value to the student of hymnology, followed by the *Hymni Ecclesiastici* of Cassander in 1556, with other works that might be named, bear witness to the desire which was felt in the Roman Catholic Church to preserve its treasures of sacred song. Amongst the Protestants, Spangenberg and George Fabricius, contemporaries of Cassander, rendered similar service, collecting from a wide range of manuscript service-books much that would otherwise probably have been lost.

But in England little interest appears to have been felt in Latin hymnology. Roman Catholics continued to use such hymns as are contained in the Breviary, but the number translated into English was small. The *Primers* which from time to time were published for members of that communion in this country contained a few English versions, some of them of considerable merit, but they had no wide circulation, and it is plain that there was no great desire to popularise the old devotions of the Church. Among Protestants there was even less disposition to draw from these ancient sources, and this indifference remained unbroken until the Oxford Movement turned attention to mediæval and early hymns. It then became the fashion to exalt the Middle Ages, as they were loosely called, and while the more learned leaders of that movement were able to discriminate, after a while at least, between things that differed, the general sentiment regarded everything that was Latin as "primitive," whether it belonged, as in the case of the Paris Breviary, to the seventeenth century, or dated from the age of Hilary and Ambrose.

But amid much that was shallow and unreal in the mediævalism of the Oxford Movement there was an undoubted desire on the part of many of the devoutest minds in the Church of England to recover the centuries which had practically dropped out of memory, and to revive strains of devotion that had been long forgotten. While the theologians cried "Back to the Fathers," and ecclesiologists were studying ritual, there arose a succession of men more or less gifted with poetic powers who translated the newly-discovered Latin hymns into English with such success that they not only took swift possession of the Church of England, but were received, after a little hesitation, into the hymn books of all the Churches. In less than two generations they have become an unquestioned and much-prized portion of the Church song of the English-speaking world.

But nothing from this source was available when the *Supplement* to the Methodist Hymn Book was compiled in 1830. No one could then foresee the profound and far-reaching influence of a movement that was gathering its forces but had not yet revealed its character, and which, in its earlier stages, would be regarded as only evil. One after another, and then in clusters, writers like Bishop Mant, Isaac Williams, and Dr. Neale and Dr.

Newman, Copeland, Chandler, Caswall, and Sir Henry Baker gave new life and form to hymns which, outside the Roman Communion, and, to a large extent, within it, had been forgotten; and one after another the Protestant Churches, Methodist, Presbyterian, and Congregational, received the best of them into their hymn books, to the enrichment of their devotional life and public worship.

The compilers of the *Supplement* of 1830 had no question of Latin hymns before them, and if they had would probably have met it with a prompt refusal even to consider it; but the revisers of the Hymn Book of 1876 could no more pass these by than they could ignore the purely English hymnody of the preceding thirty years. They say in their preface, "Our age is richer in good hymns than any that have gone before it," and their selection shows that they included among these good hymns many translations from the Latin. Among the ancients whom they welcomed are Ambrose, the two Bernards, Thomas of Celano, and Godescalcus; and they are accompanied and introduced by Neale and Caswall, by Dr. Irons and Sir Walter Scott.

I may say frankly that I wish they had drawn more freely from this source, even had it involved the necessity of going without some other hymns which came into the Wesleyan Hymn Book at its last revision. There is, for example, Dr. Ray Palmer's translation from Bernard of Clairvaux, "Jesu, Thou joy of loving hearts," which well might have accompanied Caswall's lovely hymn from the same original. There is, again, the Rev. J. Chandler's version of the Ambrosian *Jesu, nostra Redemptio*, "Jesu, our Hope, our heart's desire," and others that might be named.

The diseases by which the hymnody of the Latin Church was, in course of time, weakened and vitiated are sufficiently known — the worship paid to the Virgin Mary, the superstitious devotions offered to departed saints, the gross materialism into which sacramental doctrine sank. All this wrought havoc with the Church's hymnody, as it did with its spiritual life. But there still survives a body of pure and noble Latin hymns of much greater extent than the specimens contained in the Wesleyan Hymn Book would suggest. Meanwhile, a few notes on the latter will not be without interest to those who are familiar with the historic collection into which they have been introduced.

CHAPTER II.

The "Te Deum."

THE hymns of Latin origin in the Wesleyan Hymn Book now in use are thirteen in number, and it will be convenient to give a list of them before proceeding to discuss their history and character. They are as follows:

647-649 "Infinite God, to Thee we raise," *Te Deum* (Unknown), C. Wesley.
663 "The strain upraise of joy and praise" (Godescalcus), Dr. Neale.
680 "Jesu, the very thought of Thee" (Bernard of Clairvaux), E. Caswall.
690 "O come, O come, Immanuel" (Unknown), Dr. Neale.
751 "Come, Holy Ghost, our souls inspire" (Uncertain), Bishop Cosin.
752 "Creator Spirit, by whose aid" (Uncertain), J. Dryden.
753 "Holy Ghost! my Comforter" (Uncertain, ascribed to King Robert II. of France), Miss Winkworth.
869 "Disposer Supreme, and Judge of the earth" (Santeuil), Isaac Williams.
933 "Day of wrath! O day of mourning!" (Thomas of Celano), Dr. Irons.
934 "The day of wrath, that dreadful day" (Thomas of Celano), Sir Walter Scott.

THE "TE DEUM."

943 "Brief life is here our portion" (Bernard of Clugny), Dr. Neale.
966 "Once more the sun is beaming bright" (Ambrose), J. Chandler.
991 "Christ is our Corner-stone" (Unknown), J. Chandler.

Hymn 647-649, a metrical version of the *Te Deum* by Charles Wesley, is not, properly speaking, a translation from the Latin, but a free paraphrase of a translation, that, viz., which is found in the English Prayer Book. The hymn, *Te Deum Laudamus*, is, beyond all controversy, the greatest and most famous of Christian hymns. For nearly 1,400 years it has been used in the Sunday morning service of the Western Church, and is, perhaps, not less prized in the communities that have discarded liturgical forms than in those that retain them. Its vitality is that of an immortal. Sung more frequently than any other hymn, alike in rude and dark ages and in those of amplest light and most advanced civilisation, in cathedrals and in village chapels, at the coronation of kings and at humblest festivals, it has lost nothing of its dignity, strength, and sweetness by lapse of time or frequent use, and will continue, we may confidently say, to be the Church's chief hymn till the worship of earth shall merge in that of heaven. It is hardly less a creed than a prayer or song of praise, and the reformed and unreformed Churches unite in it as in a confession of faith.

Everyone who has even a slight knowledge of Latin should make acquaintance with the original. The Prayer Book version is itself a masterpiece, and when compared with later metrical versions its stately English and grave rhythmic beauty are at once apparent; but the dignity and sweetness of the Latin are impressive and touching in the highest degree, while in more than one instance the translation leaves something to be desired in respect of accuracy.

The author of this great hymn is unknown. We may give a kindly dismissal to the legend that it sprang by sudden inspiration from the lips of Ambrose and Augustine at the baptism of the latter in the Church of St. John at Milan. The legend has poetic charm, and a certain fitness, as long as it is not taken literally.

But in making Ambrose cry "*Te Deum laudamus, Te Dominum confitemur*," and Augustine reply "*Te Æternum Patrem omnis terra veneratur*," and so on, antiphonally, to the end, we recognise the working of the same tendency as in the legend of the origin of the Apostles' Creed, which represents the Apostles meeting together to agree upon articles of faith, when Peter begins "I believe in God the Father Almighty," and Andrew continues, "And in Jesus Christ His only Son," and so on to Matthias, who contributes the last two words, "life everlasting." This class of pious stories, not in the first place, perhaps, meant to be taken literally, was quite to the mediæval mind; "magnificent," we may say, "but not—*history*."

Passing by the legend of Ambrose and Augustine as joint authors of the *Te Deum*, the claims of Hilary of Poitiers, Hilary of Arles, and others need not detain us; all that can be said with tolerable certainty is that the *Te Deum*, as we now have it, belongs to the first half of the fifth century, and that it probably originated in Southern Gaul. But who wrote it we cannot tell. Like the so-called Athanasian Creed, its author or authors remain unknown, hidden in impenetrable obscurity from the eyes of after generations. It is to a nameless benefactor the Christian Church owes its chief hymn of praise, as it owes many another gift in its treasury.

Wesley's version is, as I have said, not a translation, but a paraphrase, and that with such expansion that the 193 words of the original are represented by 517 in English. A comparison of the first verse of Wesley's hymn with the first two sentences of the Latin to which they correspond will serve to illustrate the kind of amplification which prevails throughout. Here is the original:

> "Te Deum laudamus: Te Dominum confitemur.
> Te Æternum Patrem omnis terra veneratur";

which may be translated:

> "Thee, God, we praise: Thee as Lord we acknowledge.
> Thee the eternal Father all the earth doth worship."

And here is Wesley's paraphrase:

> "Infinite God, to Thee we raise
> Our hearts in solemn songs of praise;
> By all Thy works on earth adored,
> We worship Thee, the common Lord;
> The everlasting Father own,
> And bow our souls before Thy throne."

Here the word *laudamus* is rendered by "we raise our hearts in solemn songs of praise," and "bow ourselves before Thy throne" has nothing in the original to correspond with it. Further, "Infinite," as applied to God, and "common," as a predicate of Lord, are not translations, but additions to the original.

It is not necessary to pursue the comparison. Wesley did not place himself under the restraints of a translator, whose primary duty is to take nothing from and add nothing to the original. His was a freer, a less fettered task. Following in the main the line of thought in the English prose version, he aims at producing it in metrical form with such expansions, additions, or variations as he may think best for purposes of edification, and the result is a hymn which, though it has very great merits, gives little idea of the special characteristics of form and proportion, of tone and key, that belong to the original.

Wesley does not appear to have gone behind the English Prayer Book version, even for purposes of reference or comparison, or he would hardly have given us the line:

> "Head of the martyrs' noble host."

How the word *noble* found its way into the English version, so that "*Martyrum* candidatus *exercitus*" should be rendered "The *noble* army of martyrs," is very difficult to explain.

In the word "*candidatus*," white-robed, there is unmistakable reference to Rev. vi. 11, "And white robes were given unto every one of them"; and vii. 13, 14, "These are they which came out of great tribulation, and have washed their robes and made them white in the blood of the Lamb." The word, indeed, came to have a well understood significance in Christian Latin. The classical "*candidatus*," or white-toga'd seeker of office (candidate), gives place in the vocabulary of the Church to the *"candidatus,"* or confessor of Christ, to whom the white robe of victory and joy had been awarded after suffering. Prudentius speaks of Christ as presiding over the white-robed bands (*"candidatis præsidet cohortibus"*), and, in at least one passage, uses the word as equivalent to martyr: " Remember, O city, thou art hallowed by thrice six martyrs " (*" ter senis sacra candidatis "*).

In all translations of the *Te Deum* down to the sixteenth century the special meaning of the word, surely a beautiful and precious one, appears to have been preserved. The Greek, the Anglo-Saxon, the German, the Old French (*" le enblanchi ost des martirs "*) all keep close to the original. In early English versions we have "the white host of martyrs," and later, "the fair fellowship of martyrs," but from the middle of the sixteenth century the word "noble" has stood where it now stands, and the associations of the original have been lost.

The *Dictionary of Hymnology* gives a list of no fewer than twenty-seven English metrical versions of the *Te Deum*, all, or nearly all, based upon the Prayer Book version. The earliest of them is taken from the *Old Version* of the Psalms, by Sternhold and Hopkins, published in 1560, and as it is not now easily accessible to the general reader, I may quote a part of it:

> "We praise Thee, God, we knowledge Thee
> The only Lord to be,
> And as eternal Father all
> The earth doth worship Thee:
> To Thee all angels cry, the heavens
> And all the powers therein:
> To Thee cherub and seraphin
> To cry they do not lin.
>
> "The noble and victorious host
> Of martyrs sound Thy praise:
> The holy Church throughout the world
> Doth knowledge Thee always.
> Father of endless majesty,
> They do acknowledge Thee
> Thy Christ, Thine honourable, true,
> And only Son to be."

In later editions of the *Old Version*, while the Psalms remained unchanged, the *Te Deum* is somewhat modernised. The archaic word "lin" disappears, and the couplet reads:

> "To Thee incessantly do cry
> Cherub and seraphin."

In the *New Version* of Tate and Brady (1696, published with supplement 1703) the verse is smoother, and of the type which will always be associated with the eighteenth century:

> "O God, we praise Thee and confess
>   That Thou the only Lord
> And everlasting Father art,
>   By all the earth adored.
> To Thee all angels cry aloud;
>   To Thee the Powers on high,
> Both cherubim and seraphim,
>   Continually do cry.
> The Apostles' glorious company,
>   And Prophets crowned with light,
> With all the martyrs' noble host
>   Thy constant praise recite."

No metrical version of the *Te Deum*, however, neither Charles Wesley's nor any other, has gained a hold upon English speaking people to be compared for a moment with that of the noble prose version of the Prayer Book. The "Bible English" of that version, at once strong, sweet, and stately, the rhythmic sentences sweeping onward from the first cry of adoration to the last prayer for safe keeping, indispose us to change them for rhymed stanzas, with their inevitable expansions and dilutions. The instinct in this respect is the same in the cathedral and the conventicle, and we shall doubtless continue to sing the *Te Deum* in the form that time has sanctioned and a thousand associations have endeared.

Amongst metrical versions, however, there is none superior to Charles Wesley's, hardly any other indeed which has taken, or retains, hold on Christian congregations. There is a version by Dryden, first published by Sir Walter Scott in his life of the poet, which, though utterly unsuited for use in public worship, is interesting for those vigorous qualities that characterise Dryden's serious verse. Here are the opening stanzas:

> "Thee, Sovereign God, our grateful accents praise;
> We own Thee Lord, and bless Thy wondrous ways;
> To Thee, Eternal Father, earth's whole frame,
> With loudest trumpets, sounds immortal fame.
> Lord God of Hosts! for Thee the heavenly powers,
> With sounding anthems, fill the vaulted towers."

The following stanzas are well in Dryden's

manner, but, how far removed from the spirit of the original!

> "Legions of Martyrs in the chorus shine,
> And vocal blood with vocal music join.
> By these Thy Church, inspired by heavenly art,
> Around the world maintains a second part:
> And tunes her sweetest notes, O God, to Thee,
> The Father of unbounded majesty."
>
> * * * * *
>
> Old tyrant Death disarmed, before Thee flew
> The bolts of heaven, and back the folding drew."

It is not to be wondered at that this noble hymn has not escaped the corrupt and superstitious uses to which the best things have been exposed. Legends of a trivial and unworthy character replaced the devout and sober tributes to its worth which earlier ages had rendered. It is said, for instance, that the heart of St. Augustine of Lyons, preserved in a golden reliquary, would throb when the *Te Deum* was sung. A Jesuit writer affirms that at the sound of the *Te Deum* sung at sea, "the dolphins came together in troops, swimming round the ship, and accompanying it for a great distance."

But the crowning instance of wicked and foolish perversion is to be found in the *Canticum Marianum* of Bonaventura, who composed a version of the *Te Deum* in honour of the Virgin Mary, *Te Matrem Dei laudamus*. It is only right to say that it remains a prayer "of private devotion," and has never been admitted into public worship. I will translate a few stanzas of it from my copy of the *Psalterium Marianum* of the Seraphic Doctor St. Bonaventura, published at the office of the *De Propagandâ Fide*, Rome, 1873:

" We praise thee, Mother of God ; we acknowledge thee the
    Virgin Mary.
Thee the daughter of the Eternal Father all the earth doth
    worship
Thee all angels and archangels, thrones and principalities
    faithfully serve.
Thee all powers and heavenly virtues, and universal domin-
    ations obey,
To thee all angels cry aloud,
Holy, Holy, Holy, Mother of God, both Mother and
    Virgin."

But this is surely enough.

CHAPTER III.

Veni, Creator Spiritus.

THE Wesleyan Hymn Book contains two English versions of this great and notable hymn (751 and 752), following in this respect the Prayer Book of the Church of England, which, omitting all other hymns found in earlier service books, has retained the *Veni, Creator Spiritus*, in a shorter and a longer version, in its form for the ordering of priests, and again in that for the consecration of a bishop. To these and other English versions I shall refer later on, but the hymn itself in its original form calls first for our attention.

It is emphatically one of the great hymns of Western Christendom. Alike by its contents and its form—Scriptural without a single false note in doctrine or devotion, and in style and versification grave, simple, and restrained—

it belongs to the highest class of Latin hymns, and illustrates their characteristic merits. Who wrote it no one knows, as the student who has patience to examine the literature of the subject will soon be persuaded. No direct evidence is available, and the possibilities and probabilities of the case are differently judged by different writers. The popular favourite is the Emperor Charles the Great (Charlemagne), but the story on which his claim is mainly based breaks down upon examination. It belongs to the same class of legends as that which associates Ambrose and Augustine in the production of the *Te Deum*, and, like that charming story, may be enjoyed without being taken seriously. When, however, Fabricius ascribes it to Ambrose, Wackernagel and Mone to Gregory, Daniel to Charlemagne, and Duffield to Rabanus Maurus, Archbishop of Mainz in the middle of the ninth century, it is clear that the question is hardly likely to be settled. Sober scholars like Trench, Julian, and the Abbé Pimont are content to leave the authorship undetermined. But it has been in use since the tenth century, and the echoes of a still earlier period may be heard in it. I will venture to quote it in full, both for its own sake, and to facilitate comparison between the original and certain translations :

I.

"Veni, Creator Spiritus,
　Mentes tuorum visita,
　Imple supernâ gratiâ
　Quæ Tu creasti pectora.

II.

"Qui Paraclitus diceris,
　Donum Dei Altissimi,
　Fons vivus, ignis, charitas,
　Et spiritalis unctio.

III.

"Tu Septiformis munere,
　Dextræ Dei Tu digitus,
　Tu rite promissum Patris,
　Sermone ditans guttura.

IV.

"Accende lumen sensibus,
　Infunde amorem cordibus,
　Infirma nostri corporis
　Virtute firmans perpetim.

V.

"Hostem repellas longius
 Pacemque dones protinus
 Ductore sic Te prævio
 Vitemus omne noxium.

VI.

"Per te sciamus da Patrem,
 Noscamus atque filium,
 Te utriusque Spiritum.
 Credamus omni tempore."

It may be convenient to offer a literal prose translation to assist the reader in judging of the closeness, or otherwise, of the metrical translations he may wish to compare with the original.

1. Come, Creator Spirit, visit the minds of Thy people, fill with Divine grace the souls which Thou hast made.

2. Thou who art called Paraclete, gift of God Most High, living Fount, Fire, Love, and spiritual unction.

3. Thou sevenfold in gift, Thou Finger of God's right Hand, Thou solemn promise of the Father, endowing the lips with speech.

4. Bring light to our understanding, fill our hearts with love, the weakness of our flesh continually strengthening with might.

5. Drive far our foe, and straightway give peace, that so with Thee for guide we may flee every hurtful thing.

6. Grant us through Thee to know the Father, to know also the Son, and Thee the Spirit of each to believe for evermore.

The hymn is, it will be seen, a prayer to the Holy Spirit. The term *Creator*, which rules the entire strain, has reference to the second creation, the new birth of which the Spirit is the Author, "*created* in Christ Jesus." Each of the other designations under which the Spirit is invoked has its Biblical justification, easily verified. The living water, the fire, the love shed abroad in the heart, the unction of the Holy One, "the seven Spirits of God" in the Apocalypse, the "Finger of God" by which Christ cast out devils, are all familiar to the reader of the New Testament as descriptions of the Spirit's working, or as modes of His manifestation.

The note of supplication, sounded in the first word of the hymn, *Veni*, "Come," vibrates throughout. Although "the Spirit of truth" is "come," and no second coming of the Comforter is to be looked for, except as bound up with that of our Lord Himself, yet "Come, Holy Ghost," is the ever renewed prayer of the Church and of the Christian soul, and will continue to be so as long as the conflict with evil lasts. Nothing can be more simple and direct than the strain of petition. There are no ingenuities, no rhetorical amplifications, no looking round, so to speak, while addressing God. The variety of names and titles assigned to the Holy Spirit express intensity and importunity of prayer, for each of them has its accompanying promises, or gives ground of hope to the suppliant. At a later period the stream of devotion spent itself to a lamentable extent in adoration, not to say adulation, poured at the feet of the Virgin Mary, but here no human form is in view, and the prayer ascends without intermediary to the Third Person of the Holy Trinity. It is the prototype of a class of hymns expressing the most spiritual desires of the Christian soul, hymns without which the Church's supplications would indeed be incomplete. For well nigh a thousand years it has been counted a chief jewel in the Church's treasury of devotion, brought out at the coronation of kings and the ordination of clergy, and dear also to humble and lowly hearts seeking light and grace and cleansing in private or in public prayer.

One of its earliest translators says of it, "Whoever repeats this hymn by day or night, no enemy, visible or invisible, shall assail him." "It is a hymn," says Guéranger, in his *Année Liturgique*, "for ever new, and for ever inexhaustible." And the Abbé Pimont, a distinguished French hymnologist, pays it the following tribute: "It is impossible to listen to it without being moved to the very depths of the soul, and being surrounded, as it were, by that mysterious atmosphere in which God is pleased to speak to the heart when He would subdue it by His grace."

The two versions in the Wesleyan Hymn Book come now to be considered. "Come, Holy Ghost, our souls inspire" (751), was written by John Cosin, Bishop of Durham. It first appeared in his *Collection of Private Devotions*, published in 1627, when Cosin was Rector of Brancepeth, and afterwards in the Prayer Book of 1662, that is, the Prayer Book

VENI, CREATOR SPIRITUS.

as it now exists. Up to that time the Prayer Book had contained a much longer version of the *Veni Creator*, so long, indeed, that a shorter one was felt to be necessary; Bishop Cosin's translation was added as an alternative, and the two have stood together ever since in the forms for the Ordering of Priests and the Consecration of Bishops, the one containing eighteen lines, and the other no fewer than sixty-four. The longer hymn, especially in the form in which it appears in the Prayer Book of Edward VI., is rough and quaint, but not without charm, as the following stanzas will show:

> "Thou in Thy gifts art manifold,
>   Whereby Christ's Church doth stand,
> In faithful hearts writing Thy law,
>   The finger of God's hand:
> According to Thy promise made,
>   Thou givest speech of grace,
> That through Thy help the praise of God
>   May sound in every place.
>
> " Put back our enemy far from us,
>   And grant us to obtain
> Peace in our hearts with God and man,
>   Without grudge or disdain.

> And grant, O Lord, that Thou being
> Our leader and our guide,
> We may eschew the snares of sin,
> And from Thee never slide."

Bishop Cosin's version is a hymn of rare excellence. Vigorous, without being harsh or uncouth, packing the utmost meaning in fewest words, brief and strong as the Latin itself, it has, I think, no superior, if, indeed, an equal, of its kind. Particular phrases of it pass into the memory and dwell there:

> "Thy blessed unction from above,
> Is comfort, life, and fire of love."

And again:

> "Keep far our foes, give peace at home,
> Where Thou art guide no ill can come."

Where can one find thought, feeling, and expression more completely fused and compacted?

It is not a literal translation: it is something rarer and better. The spirit of the Latin original would seem to have wrought for itself an English form, not caring to reproduce each feature of its first creation, but shaping another like it.

Hymn 752, "Creator Spirit, by whose aid,' is linked with a great name, that of John Dryden, Poet Laureate from 1670 till the accession of William III. in 1688. He became a Roman Catholic in 1685. Of his versatility —achieving the highest distinction of his time in every province of literature—nothing need here be said. His intellectual force, his command of language, his mastery alike of prose and verse, and a certain stateliness of character that belonged to him, are well known. The indelible stain upon his memory, the blot which no revision or abridgment can remove from his writings, is the gross immorality of his dramas. For more than thirty years Dryden was writing for the stage, and this long connection with the theatre involved a moral degradation that can hardly be exaggerated — to himself nothing less than dishonour, and to English literature a lasting injury. To use Mr. Lowell's phrase, "One has to hold one's nose while picking one's way through the nastiness of his pages." The obscenity of his plays is, in a sense, the less excusable, and at the same time the less comprehensible, because Dryden does not appear to have been a man of unclean mind or dissolute habits. The licentiousness of the stage after the Restoration was an evil fashion, and Dryden fell in with it. The King and the Court were as worthless a set as the world ever saw—selfish, unprincipled, and shameless, and it seemed to be the ambition of the dramatists to put upon the stage characters as profane and indecent as they were. Dryden's share in this evil business offends us more than that of anyone else. When base men do base things we recognise a kind of fitness in things, and disgust and contempt are our predominant feelings. But when one who is better bred, and has shown himself capable of better things, betakes himself to the gutter and the dunghill, our disgust becomes sorrow and indignation. There was undoubtedly another and a nobler strain in Dryden. He was no hypocrite, and the hymns which he wrote assuredly express sentiments and convictions which he sincerely held. Such are the anomalies that human character presents, such the inconsistencies which human nature can exhibit in the imperfect balance of good and evil in the soul.

Until recently but three hymns were assigned to Dryden, all of them translations from the Latin; but recent investigation has shown with something approaching to certainty that he translated upwards of a hundred hymns, contained in the Roman Catholic *Primer* of 1706. Much interesting information on this subject is given by Mr. Orby Shipley in the Preface to his *Annus Sanctus*. All these would be written during the last fifteen years of his life, and such an employment suggests a change in the poet's mind that we are glad to believe in. Not long before his death he wrote, " I have been myself too much a libertine in most of my poems, which I should be well contented I had time either to purge or to see them fairly burned."

Wesley did not feel himself prohibited from adapting Dryden's version of the *Veni Creator* for congregational purposes, and he included it in the abbreviated form with which we are familiar in his *Psalms and Hymns*, 1741. He did not, however, retain it in his Hymn Book of 1779; but since its insertion in the Supplement of 1830, it has been frequently sung and much prized by Methodist congregations. It is, indeed, a noble hymn. The original underlies it, but the translator has claimed latitude and freedom for his English version, and has given fine paraphrases of the terse Latin. "Dextræ Dei Tu Digitus" broadens out into:

> "Thou strength of His almighty Hand
> Whose power doth heaven and earth command."

"Hostem repellas longius," etc., becomes:

> "Chase from our minds the infernal foe,
> And peace, the fruit of love, bestow;
> And, lest our feet should step astray,
> Protect and guide us in the way."

Wesley's version is a very happy instance of revision and amendment applied to a hymn, a delicate undertaking only justified by success.

VENI, CREATOR SPIRITUS.

The principal variations are the following:

DRYDEN.

"Come, visit every pious mind,"
"O Source of uncreated light."
"But, oh, inflame and fill our hearts."
"Our frailties help, our vice control,
  Submit the senses to the soul."

WESLEY.

"Come, visit every *waiting* mind,"
"O Source of uncreated *heat*."
"*Refine and purge* our *earthly parts*,"
"*Create all new*; our *wills control*,
  Subdue the *rebel in our soul*."

Wesley also omits the following lines:

"Proceeding Spirit, our defence,
  Who dost the gifts of tongues dispense,
  And crownest Thy gifts with eloquence."

This strikes us as weak and diffuse.

The following couplets are vigorous, but Wesley, in his recasting of the hymn, could afford to omit them.

"(Submit the senses to the soul),
  And when rebellious they are grown,
  Then lay Thy hand, and hold them down."

And again:

> "Make us eternal truths receive,
> And practise all that we believe."

The extent to which the *Veni Creator* has passed into the devotions of English-speaking Christians may be gathered from the fact that the *Dictionary of Hymnology* gives a list of no fewer than sixty-one English versions, more than half of them composed within the last fifty years. Among the translators are Faber and Caswall, Dr. Irons, Isaac Williams, Chambers and Copeland. Amid the distractions and divisions of Christendom it is cheering to think that this prayer to the Holy Spirit, "the Lord and Giver of life," is used continually in the churches of the Roman and Anglican Communions, and in Presbyterian, Methodist, Congregational, and other assemblies of the Catholic Church, one and indivisible, in spite of all appearances to the contrary.

CHAPTER IV.

Veni, Sancte Spiritus.

HYMN 753, "Holy Ghost! my Comforter." The *Veni, Sancte Spiritus* may well stand side by side in the Hymn Book with the *Veni, Creator Spiritus*. Like the former, it is a prayer to the Holy Spirit, without doctrinal flaw, and with a strain of devotion that not only ascends to the Lord and Giver of life, but may well be thought of as kindled by Him. If in the former there is more of strength, and of the gravity and reserve that mark the earlier Latin hymns, here there is more of sweetness and pathos, and a deeper note of conflict and sorrow. Trench calls it "the loveliest of all the hymns in the whole circle of Latin sacred poetry." Clichtoveus says: "It is above all praise . . . . and I well believe that the author (whoever he was), when he composed it, had his soul transfused by a heavenly sweetness by which, the Holy Spirit being the Author, he uttered so much sweetness in so few words."

In the Wesleyan Hymn Book, as in so many others, it is ascribed to King Robert of France (d. 1031), but the research of modern scholars vindicates the modest ignorance of Clichtoveus. *Quisquis is fuerit,* "whoever he was," is all he can say of the author. In the old collections of *Sequences* that I have examined it stands without an author's name, and in the *Liber Ecclesiasticorum Carminum* (Basileœ, 1532) it has for inscription, *Autor non constat,* "the author is unknown." Trench thinks that he can trace in this hymn the consolations and sorrows of "this meek and greatly afflicted king"; but, as it is possible to reason well from mistaken premisses, so it is easy to sustain a foregone conclusion by internal evidence of the kind he adduces. Dr. Julian is positive that King Robert never wrote the *Veni, Sancte Spiritus*, but thinks its most probable author was Pope Innocent III. Duffield, the American hymnologist, is pretty certain, both from external and internal evidence, that Hermannus Contractus, a German monk and scholar of the eleventh century, is the real author.

But if the authorship remains uncertain, we cannot go far wrong in determining the period of its origin. It is a *Sequence* of the second period, which began about the middle of the twelfth century, when Adam of St. Victor broke away from the rhythmic prose in which this class of hymns had hitherto been cast, and adopted rhyming verse of the most varied metres. Not that rhymed Latin verse was previously unknown. Bernard of Cluny, for example, had already written his *De Contemptu Mundi* in rhyme of a peculiarly ingenious and difficult kind; though that indeed was not a hymn, or intended to be used in any way in the services of the Church. But as the past to which the classic models belonged became more and more remote, and the modern world became increasingly conscious of its own existence, the new spirit created new forms in language, in literature, and in art. Rhymed verse emerged from the disparagement under which it had lain, and was adopted as the medium for prayer and praise, for the deepest meditation and the loftiest flights of devotion. In the hands of Adam of St. Victor above all, but also in those of many a nameless poet beside, the Latin showed a flexibility and a variety and richness of metrical resources previously unknown. The domain of song, both sacred and secular, was widened, and while common life was enriched with popular verse that caught the ear and fastened on the memory, much as our own English and Scottish ballads did at a later day, from the churches and monasteries went forth a class of hymns and sacred songs delightful to hear and easy to remember.

Whoever composed the *Veni, Sancte Spiritus*, he was a master of his art, as well as a devout and enlightened soul. The scheme of versification is simple, but possesses considerable metrical charm. The hymn is of ten stanzas, each consisting of three lines of seven syllables, of which the last but one is always short. The two first lines rhyme with each other, and the third rhymes with the corresponding line of the stanza following, or, in other words, the third lines rhyme throughout, producing a pleasing effect by the recurrence of the same sound at stated intervals from the beginning to the end. Let the reader pronounce each syllable distinctly, giving to the vowels their broad and open sound, and in the case of double consonants duly emphasising each, and he will have a fair idea of the rhythmical qualities of the hymn.

> "Veni, Sancte Spiritus,
> Et emitte cœlitus
> Lucis tuæ radium.
>
> "Veni, pater pauperum,
> Veni, dator munerum,
> Veni, lumen cordium.
>
> "Consolator optime,
> Dulcis hospes animæ,
> Dulce refrigerium.
>
> "In labore requies,
> In æstu temperies,
> In fletu solatium.

VENI, SANCTE SPIRITUS.

"O lux beatissima,
  Reple cordis intima
  Tuorum fidelium.

"Sine tuo numine
  Nihil est in homine,
  Nihil est innoxium.

"Lava quod est sordidum,
  Riga quod est aridum,
  Sana quod est saucium.

"Flecte quod est rigidum,
  Fove quod est frigidum,
  Rege quod est devium.

"Da tuis fidelibus,
  In te confidentibus
  Sacrum septenarium.

"Da virtutis meritum,
  Da salutis exitum,
  Da perenne gaudium."

It will be observed that the rhymes are double and triple rhymes (Spiritus . . . Cœlitus; rigidum . . . frigidum, etc.), never single ones (dearth . . . worth; quest, best, etc.) The difference between the Latin and the English modes of inflection makes it both difficult and undesirable to use such rhymes in an English version, and the best translators do not attempt it, but seek to reproduce the effect of the original by other means. This is most skilfully and successfully accomplished in Miss Winkworth's version, hymn 753. The three-line stanza and the seven-syllable trochaic line are here, and instead of a recurring rhyme carried through the entire hymn, each verse is rhythmically complete within itself.

The closeness of rendering and the reproduction of the spirit of the original are the more remarkable as Miss Winkworth's version is a translation of a translation, a German version given in Bunsen's Collection. But the result is an English hymn of great excellence—gracious, tender, and truly supplicatory, charged throughout with holy longing expressed in pure and simple language. As in all, or nearly all, translations there is now and again an expansion of the original; but where the key is maintained, and the expansion is within the limits of good taste and the sense of proportion, it must be accepted. There is also the occasional failure to reproduce a distinctive thought, and substitute some other that is less definite.

The sixth verse is a good instance of the amplification to which a translator is almost driven by the terseness of the original. It may be rendered:

> "Without Thy divinity
> Nothing is in man,
> Nothing is harmless."

In the Latin the iteration, *nihil-nihil*, is impressive from its brevity and absoluteness. Miss Winkworth's expansion of the thought:

> "What without Thy aid is wrought,
> Skilful deed or wisest thought,
> God will count but vain and nought,"

is also impressive, but the strain of thought is more complex, and the emotion is, so to speak, spread over a wider area. It is interesting to compare other English versions of this stanza. The following are the best with which I am acquainted:

> "For, without Thy sacred powers,
> Nothing can we own of ours,
> Nothing undefiled."—Mrs. Charlesworth.

> "If Thou take Thy grace away
> Nothing pure in man will stay,
> All his good is turn'd to ill."—E. Caswall.

> "If Thy Deity be hence
> Nothing brings man honour thence—
> Nothing is without offence."—R. Campbell.

> "Without thy Godhead nothing can
> Have any price or worth in man,
> Nothing can harmless be."
> —Service Book, 1763.

Comparisons of this kind will well repay the student alike of literature and of theology. Here, for example, are five different ways of rendering *sine tuo numine* and *nihil est innoxium*, involving delicacies of interpretation and expression which need not be further considered here, but in which a student may find exercise and advantage.

A very striking expression in the original (verse 2), *Veni, pater pauperum*, is lost in our Hymn Book version. "Father of the poor" is a remarkable designation of the Holy Spirit. It cannot have been accidental, but evidently stands for some aspect of the Holy Spirit's office that was present to the writer's mind. It suggests the *Beati pauperes* of the Sermon on the Mount, and "the Father of mercies, and God of all consolation," of St. Paul.

Corner, in his *Cantica Selecta* (Lipsiæ, 1568), has a note to this effect: "Because like a father He hears and cares for the poor in spirit."

In the ninth verse the English paraphrase is vaguer than was necessary. *Sacrum septenarium*, "the sevenfold gifts of the Spirit," is an expression so well established in mediæval theology that it would have been well to indicate its presence here. This is done in other versions, as, for instance:

> "To Thine own in every place
> Give the sacred sevenfold grace,
> Give Thy faithful this."
> —Mrs. Charlesworth.

> "Thou, on those who evermore
> Thee confess and Thee adore,
> In Thy sevenfold gifts, descend."
> —E. Caswall.

> "Unto us who seek Thy face,
> And in Thee reliance place,
> Give Thy sevenfold gifts of grace."
> —R. Campbell.

But these criticisms, if such they may be called, must not be taken in disparagement of the beautiful hymn for which we are indebted to the authoress of the *Lyra Germanica*. It is sufficiently close to its original—one of the great, enduring hymns of Western Christendom—and has a grace and sweetness of its own. It will keep its place among the best of the hymns — not too numerous — in which the Christian pleads with the ever-blessed Spirit for light and cleansing, for sanctity and peace.

The *Dictionary of Hymnology* gives a list of thirty-seven English versions of the *Veni, Sancte Spiritus*. That by Caswall appears to be the most widely used, though greatly altered by different editors and revisers. The version in *Hymns Ancient and Modern* is one of these, and the compilers have allowed themselves great latitude. Neale's translation in *The Hymnal Noted* bears all the marks of his accomplished hand. As might be expected, he carries the third line rhyme, or assonance, through the entire hymn, keeping as close as possible to the rhythmic structure of the original, save that he wisely employs single rhymes for the other two lines of each stanza.

If these notes are not unduly detaining the reader, I should like to close them with a little known version of this hymn by the late Philip Stanhope Worsley, a fine scholar, a true poet, and a pure soul, whom I remember when he was a scholar of Corpus Christi College, Oxford, the friend and companion of another scholar of that College very near and dear to me.

"Come, O Holy Spirit, come;
　Earthward from Thy heavenly home
　　Flash the glowing radiance bright.

"Come, Thou Father of the poor;
　Come, Thou Giver of good store;
　　Come, of hearts Thou sovran light.

"Comforter the truest, best,
　Who the soul with pleasant rest
　　Pleasantly dost entertain;

"Ease in toil and cordial sweet,
　Shelter in the burning heat,
　　Soothing influence in pain.

"O most blessed, blessed Light,
　Shine with splendour pure and white,
　　Shine upon Thy saints within;

VENI, SANCTE SPIRITUS.

"For in man, without Thy grace,
  Nothing ever can have place,
    Nothing void of shame and sin.

"Wash to whiteness every stain,
  Slake the thirsty soil with rain,
    Heal the hurt that needs Thy care;

"Bend the stubborn to Thy sway,
  Cheer the cold with genial day,
    Make the crooked straight and clear.

"Holy Spirit, to the just,
  Who in Thee believe and trust,
    Give the sacred Sabbath rest;

"Give the guerdon they have won,
  Give supreme salvation's crown,
    Give the ages ever blest."

CHAPTER V.

Charlemagne and King Robert of France.

BEFORE passing on to the next in our series of Latin hymns, I propose to add a few notes to the last two chapters, which, it may be remembered, had to do with the *Veni, Creator Spiritus*, and the *Veni, Sancte Spiritus*.

The authorship of the former, as was previously remarked, is popularly ascribed to Charlemagne, though on entirely inadequate grounds, and, indeed, contrary to all evidence. But to assign it to the great monarch and statesman was quite in accord with prevailing sentiment. The character and history of Carolus Magnus deeply impressed the imagination of Christendom, and a great body of legend grew up around his name. It was difficult to exaggerate the greatness of his plans, of his powers, and of his achievements. In the calendar of the Roman Church he is a "Saint," and the historic designation of "the Great" was never bestowed or received with better right. On such a character and such a career as his the spirit of romance was sure to fasten, and in the poetry of the Middle Ages he appears as a being of superhuman strength and beauty, with eyes like the morning star, accompanied by a bodyguard of immortals. He died in January, 814, in the seventy-first year of his age, and the forty-seventh of his reign, and was buried at Aquis Granum (Aixla-Chapelle), *maximo totius populi luctu*, amid the greatest lamentations of the whole people.

A striking indication of the grief and dismay caused by the death of this mighty ruler of men is afforded by an anonymous poem written almost immediately afterwards, *Chant sur la mort de Charlemagne*, of which I will give the first verse as a specimen, together with a rough translation of the whole :

"A solis ortu usque ad occidua
   Littora maris, planctus pulsat pectora;
   Ultra maria agmina tristitia
   Tetigit ingens cum mœrore nimis,
       Heu! me dolens, plango."

"From the sun's rising even to the western
   Shores of ocean they are beating their breasts;
   The folk over sea a burden of sorrow
   Oppresses with grief overwhelming.
       Ah! woe is me.

"Franks and Romans, yea, all of the faithful
   Are smitten with mourning and utter dismay;
   Children and greybeards, princes illustrious,
   And mothers are wailing for Carolus dead.
       Ah! woe is me.

"Ceaseless are flowing their rivers of tears,
   Through the world echoes the downfall of Carolus;
   Christ, who art Lord of the cohorts of heaven,
   Grant in Thy Kingdom, grant rest to Carolus.
       Ah! woe is me.

"Woe to thee, city, and people of Rome,
   Gone is thy chieftain, gone is great Carolus!
   Woe to thee, Italy, lone in thy beauty!
   At Aquis Granum in dust lies the sceptre.
       Ah! woe is me.

"O Columbanus, stay now thy weeping,
   And offer up prayers for him to the Lord!
   Father of all bereaved, Father of all
   Wayfarers, widows, and virgins!
       Ah! woe is me.

> "Night's darkness brings me no sleep,
> Nor day with its shining brings light.
> All Father, Lord of compassion,
> Grant to him high place in heaven.
> Ah me, I mourn."

I should like to believe that Carolus Magnus wrote the *Veni, Creator Spiritus*, but am unable.

As to the supposed royal author of *Veni, Sancte Spiritus*, King Robert the Second of France, though Trench accepts the tradition of his authorship without question, I fear he, too, is impossible. The most recent research —and on its historical side hymnology has been greatly advanced of late years—makes it very doubtful whether he wrote any one of the five hymns that have been attributed to him, and almost certain that he did not write this one in particular. The *Dictionary of Hymnology* thinks that possibly the Sequence, *Rex omnipotens, die hodiernâ*, was his, but Kehrein assigns it, not very confidently however, to Hermannus Contractus. It is a "prose" of the earlier order on the Ascension of our Lord :

"Rex omnipotens, die hodiernâ,
   Mundo triumphali redempto potentiâ,
   Victor ascendit cœlos, unde descenderat."

A translation will serve to show how much of evangelical truth and doctrine was preserved in Church song of this kind during the long period that preceded printed books, and during the subsequent period when the Church did not encourage the laity to read the Gospel for themselves:

"This day the King omnipotent,
   Having redeemed the world by His triumphant might,
   Ascends a Conqueror to heaven, whence He had come.
   Through forty holy days after He rose He tarried,
   Confirming the souls of the Apostles;
   To whom, bequeathing the sweet kiss of peace,
   He gave the power to bind and loose,
   And sent them to baptize all men
   In the mercy of Father, Son, and Holy Spirit.
   And, eating with them, bade them not depart
   From Jerusalem, but wait for the promised gifts.
   Not many days hence will I send to you the Spirit, the Comforter,
   And ye shall be My witnesses in Jerusalem, Judea, and Samaria.
   And when He had this said, while they beheld He rose, and a bright cloud
   Received Him from their sight, they gazing upward.

Behold, two men, in white robes clad, stood by, and said:
Why look ye to high heaven?
For this Jesus, who is taken from you to the right hand of
 the Father,
As He ascended so shall come, seeking His gain of the
 entrusted talent.
O God of ocean, air, and field, man whom Thou didst
 create, and whom by guile
The foe drove out of paradise, and led a captive with him
 to the abyss,
Whom by Thine own blood Thou hast redeemed, O God,
Bring back again thither whence first he fell,
To joys of paradise.
When Thou the judge, to judge the world shalt come,
Grant us, we pray Thee, everlasting joy
In the homeland of saints,
Where we all shall sing to Thee, Alleluia."

Whether King Robert composed this anthem or not I cannot tell. It possesses no great poetic merit, but it is Gospel truth in plain words, and I cannot doubt that Church song like this did much to nourish Christian souls, and preserve the Christian faith in dark days and perilous times.

CHAPTER VI.

Cantemus Cuncti Melodum.

(The strain upraise of joy and praise.)

IT is not difficult to determine the source and inspiration of this hymn. It is a variant on the 148th Psalm, which, in the Vulgate, has for its title or heading ALLELUIA, and calls for praise to God from all that He has made, "dragons and all deeps; fire and hail, snow and vapours; stormy wind fulfilling His word." In this respect it may be compared with the "Song of the Three Children," the *Benedicite* of the Apocrypha, which is retained in the Prayer Book, and has, indeed, been used in the services of the Church from, at least, the time of Athanasius.

Nor is it to be wondered at that this particular strain of devotion should again and again be heard in Christian song. "All Thy works praise Thee" is a note without which worship cannot be complete. It will be lacking whenever low and unworthy views of nature obtain, and to the persistence of such views we attribute its cessation from time to time; but with the recovery of a strong and joyous faith in God the Christian becomes the choirmaster of the waiting earth, and calls upon it to praise the Lord with all its myriad voices.

The hymn, or, to use the technical term, the *Sequence*, of which Dr. Neale has given us this admirable version, was by him ascribed to Godescalcus (Gottschalk), a monk of St. Gall, the monastery in which this form of liturgical song originated. I do not know on what grounds Neale and Daniel assign it to Godescalcus. Kehrein, in his *Lateinischen-Sequenzen*, and Chevalier, in the *Repertorium Hymnologicum*, assign it to Notker, the founder of this school of composition. Dreves, the most learned of recent hymnologists, who has lately edited the works of Godescalcus, does not include it among them, and Dr. March, the American scholar, introduces it amongst the works of unknown authors. The *Dictionary of Hymnology*, also, ascribes it to Notker, who belonged to the same monastery of St. Gall, and died in 912, some forty years before Godescalcus. The question is an interesting, but not an important, one. Notker led the way, and Godescalcus followed, in developing a class of sacred song which was destined to attain great dimensions, and exercise a powerful influence on the devotional life of the Church.

The Wesleyan Hymn Book follows Neale in adopting the authorship of Godescalcus, but makes an unfortunate error in adding "died A.D. 870." This is to confound the hymn-writer of the tenth century (died about 950) with the ninth century theologian of the same name, who ardently defended the Augustinian doctrine of predestination, and for so doing was imprisoned for twenty years in the neighbourhood of Rheims, dying in the year 868 or 869.

The original consists of twenty-one un-rhymed stanzas of unequal length, each complete in itself, and terminating with *Alleluia*, thus :

CANTEMUS CUNCTI MELODUM.

1. Cantemus cuncti melodum nunc Alleluia.
2. In laudibus æterni regis hæc plebs resultet Alleluia.
3. Hoc denique cœlestes chori cantent in altum Alleluia.
4. Hoc beatorum per prata paradisiaca psallat concentus Alleluia.

The strain of praise moves freely and joyously from first to last. The heading of the 148th Psalm might be taken to express its motive and methods. "The psalmist exhorteth the celestial, the terrestrial, and the rational creatures to praise God." The *Cantemus Cuncti melodum*, "Let us all sing praises," expands into an invitation to angels and men, to the stars of heaven, the clouds, the winds, and the lightnings, the mountains and the valleys, and all beasts and birds, to sing Alleluia to God, whose names, Eternal King and Creator, give place at the close to the last, the complete, name of the God of our salvation, *Domino Christo, Pneumatique, Trinitati Æternæ*, the Lord, the Christ, the Spirit, the Eternal Trinity.

A closer analysis gives us the following as the order in which the works of the Lord are called upon to take their part in the chorus of praise.

"The ransomed people," *plebs*, His people; as constantly in the Old Testament. "I will be your God, and ye shall be My people." The word stands, not for the inhabitants of the earth as such, but for the called and chosen.

With these the *cœlestes chori*, "the choirs that dwell on high," are bidden to join in the strain of praise. "All angels"—as the *Te Deum* has it, "the heavens and all the powers therein," and the *beatorum concentus*, the company of the blessed in paradise, together laud and magnify the Lord. Earth, paradise, heaven—the three spheres in which the glory of the Creator and Redeemer is manifested—furnish their companies of worshippers.

But all His works praise Him; therefore, let the stars in their courses, the clouds, the winds, and the lightnings say, Alleluia. The floods and storms, summer and winter, the birds and beasts, the mountains and the valleys, the ocean and the expanses of earth, all must offer "the frequent hymn." For the

Lord Almighty loves this strain. "Christ Himself approves," *comprobat Ipse Christus.*

The fourteenth stanza has a directness and intensity in the original that are hardly preserved in the English Version:

> "Nunc vos, O socii, cantate lætantes, Alleluia.
> Et vos, pueruli, respondete semper, Alleluia."

> "Come now, O brothers, sing with rejoicing, Alleluia;
> And you, O ye children, respond ever more, Alleluia."

The final stanza is *Laus Trinitati Æternæ. Alleluia! Alleluia! Alleluia.*

Dr. Neale's translation is a noble hymn of praise. Allowing for the difference in the genius of the two languages, the life and spirit of the Latin are wonderfully reproduced in English. The sixth stanza in the two versions will give a good idea of the skill and felicity of the translator:

> "Nubium cursus,
> Ventorum volatus,
> Fulgurum coruscatio,
> Et tonitruum sonitus
> Dulce consonent simul, Alleluia!"

"Ye clouds that onward sweep,
Ye winds on pinions light,
Ye thunders loud and deep,
Ye lightnings, wildly bright,
In sweet consent unite your Alleluia!"

Extreme closeness of rendering is here united with freedom and grace in a manner that could hardly be excelled. Dr. Neale speaks of his translation as "miserably inferior to the original." From the nature of the case, a translation is hardly ever equal to the original, but "The strain upraise" is a translation that has as little as possible to fear from the application of this rule.

The liturgical use of the word Alleluia may be studied in the *Dictionary of Hymnology*, and in the various works to which the reader is there referred, and also in Neale's *Mediæval Hymns*.

Having referred to Gottschalk, the ninth century theologian, I may add a few lines concerning him. His history is a very touching one. He was a Saxon by birth, the son of a Court Bern, who dedicated him to the priesthood, and sent him to be educated at the monastery of Fulda. On coming to full age Gottschalk repudiated the choice made for him when only a child, and protested against being a monk in spite of himself. But the binding character of the parental consecration of a child to monastic life was confirmed by the highest authorities, and Gottschalk's destiny was fixed. He devoted himself to theological studies, and in particular to the writings of Augustine. He ardently adopted and avowed that father's teaching respecting predestination and its allied doctrines. He was branded as a heretic, and henceforth knew no peace. He was driven from Italy, and returned to Mainz, where he was condemned (A.D. 848) by a Synod which examined his doctrine. The following year he was taken in hand by another Synod at Querci, in the diocese of Rheims. Here he was condemned as an incorrigible heretic, his writings were burnt, and he himself publicly scourged, after which he was thrown into prison, there to spend the last twenty years of his life, gaining release only by death.

Duméril, in his *Poésies Populaires Latines* (Vol. I.), prints from a manuscript in the National Library, Paris, a pathetic hymn by Gottschalk on the "Misery of Sin." The cry of this greatly afflicted soul, oppressed by men, and left alone to wrestle before God with darkness and fear, is most pathetic. It is too lengthy to quote, but a few stanzas will show its character and tone:

> "O God, have mercy
> Upon Thy miserable servant.
> Since Thou badest me be born,
> Beyond all things have I loved
> To feed upon vanity.

> "Thou didst create me
> That Thee I might serve:
> I, wretched, rebelled,
> And went far astray.

> "Thou didst redeem me
> From slavish yoke,
> And I would not know Thee
> Nor turn again home.

> "The sweet law Thou gavest
> I foolish neglected;
> The thing Thou forbadest
> I greedily followed.

> "All good things I turned from
> With loathing mind;
> All things that were evil
> I quickly laid hold on."

Then follow prayers for mercy and pardon. He implores the saints to intercede for him— Mary, St. Michael, Peter, and martyrs and virgins. To us this breaks and spoils the strain. It should be remembered, however, that Gottschalk was not scourged and imprisoned for seeking the intercession of the saints, but for holding doctrine that Calvin taught, that Jonathan Edwards defended, and Spurgeon preached. It was Augustine in him that was scourged and imprisoned.

CHAPTER VII.

Jesu, Dulcis Memoria.

(Jesu, the very thought of Thee.)

ALTHOUGH this lovely hymn is, both in its Latin and in its English form, the offspring of the cloister, such is the happy superiority of the spiritual life, when at its best, to place and circumstance, that it bears no trace of its monastic origin, and needs no revising to adapt it for universal Christian use. It is, indeed, an evangelical hymn of purest strain, unmixed with any alloy of earlier or later Romanism, the utterance of that love and longing for Christ which is one and the same among the true children of God in all ages. For centuries Bernard's hymn nourished devout souls in the Roman Church, and now for fifty years it has had the wide, free range of the English language, and is as well, if not better, known and prized outside that Church than in it. It is found in all our hymn books, it is sung in all our congregations, and is used in the inner sanctuaries of private devotion, dear alike to the learned and the simple, the old and the young.

> " Jesu, the very thought of Thee
>   With sweetness fills my breast ;
> But sweeter far Thy face to see,
>   And in Thy presence rest.
>
> " Nor voice can sing, nor heart can frame,
>   Nor can the memory find
> A sweeter sound than Thy blest Name,
>   O Saviour of mankind.
>
> " O Hope of every contrite heart,
>   O Joy of all the meek,
> To those who fall how kind Thou art !
>   How good to those who seek.
>
> " But what to those who find ? Ah ! this
>   Nor tongue, nor pen, can show ;
> The love of Jesus, what it is,
>   None but His loved ones know."

There is hardly anything in English hymnody more simple, pure, and heart-moving than this. We place these verses by the side of " Jesu, Lover of my soul," and " Rock of Ages, cleft for me." They are of the same order ; they spring from the same source; they express the same needs and longings of the soul. It is more than seven hundred years since Bernard of Clairvaux died, hardly twenty since Edward Caswall, his English translator, passed away; but day by day their voices are heard in the congregations of Christendom, sweet singers whom death does not and cannot silence. Happy the men, whatever their conflicts and sorrows, to whom it is given to provide for fellow-travellers in their own and after ages such songs in the house of their pilgrimage.

It is not necessary to recount here even the main features of Bernard's great career. He is a conspicuous figure in the history of Europe, and has had many biographers. Belonging to the Middle Ages, Bernard was the very embodiment of the noblest mediæval qualities, not unaccompanied by the defects of the time and of the order of things to which he belonged. He was a monk, an ascetic, and a scholar who had mastered the whole round of accessible learning. As the founder of a monastic order, he planted, and built, and ruled a laborious brotherhood. As a venerated and commanding personage, he gave counsel to kings and popes, and held the balance of ecclesiastical power. He preached a crusade, and all Europe answered his call. He was at once preacher and orator, scholar and statesman, recluse and man of the world. Only that age could produce this type, and in Bernard it had its most illustrious example.

At what period of his life Bernard wrote his *Jubilus Rhythmicus de nomine Jesu* cannot be ascertained. Some would from internal evidence assign it to one of the closing years of his life, when he was residing in retirement and was weary of the world. It may have been so, but inferences of this kind, unless there is historic confirmation, are precarious. Outward conditions are not so powerful that they necessarily determine the strain and key of the inner life. Many a battle song has been composed in tranquil times; many a restful psalm amid the hurry of work and warfare. There is no fixed and necessary succession in the stages of the inner life. They have laws of their own, often in striking contrast with the outward conditions. There is no reason why Bernard should wait till age and weariness were upon him before writing the lines:

> "Jesu, dulcis memoria,
> Dans vera cordi gaudia,
> Sed super mel et omnia
> Ejus dulcis Præsentia."

The hurry and eagerness of his life, its conflicts and anxieties, may well have thrown him upon the hidden sources of peace. Among kings, princes, and prelates the "sweet memory of Jesus" may well have been with him, and that "sweet Presence" his unseen companion.

Let it be noted with what accumulation of humble, happy utterance he who was reckoned a very giant among men speaks of Jesus as his only joy and rejoicing:

> "Nil canitur suavius,
> Nil auditur jucundius,
> Nil cogitatur dulcius,
> Quam Jesus Dei Filius."

> "No song so soothing,
> No sound so pleasant,
> No thought so sweet
> As Jesu's Name, dear Son of God."

This is a note of frequent recurrence in our modern hymns. We may compare with it Charles Wesley's

> "Jesus, the Name that charms our fears,"

and

> "Jesus, soft, harmonious Name,"

John Newton's

> "How sweet the Name of Jesus sounds,"

and many another. Happily this strain is neither ancient nor modern—or rather, it is both. The mode of expression has varied, but the note itself runs without ceasing through all the ages of Christian worship.

The five verses forming the well-known English hymn are taken from an original of considerable length; or, to speak more precisely, the first four verses of Caswall's translation are the first, second, third, and fifth verses of Bernard's *Jubilus Rhythmicus*. The fifth, beginning "Jesu, our only joy be Thou," is not in the original, but is taken from another source.

Trench, in his *Sacred Latin Poetry*, gives fifteen verses; Daniel and Mone, following

Fabricius and the older authorities, give versions of forty-eight or fifty stanzas.

This "Joyful Rhythm" is beautiful throughout. As Trench has well pointed out, there is a certain "want of progress" in the thought. In this respect it may be compared with Charles Wesley's "Jesu, Lover of my soul." In the one hymn, as in the other, the writer's thought seems to circle round its object, seeking again and again a centre from which it cannot get away. The "progress" is not from stage to stage of thought, but from harmony to harmony of a single note which holds alike the ear and the heart. And through the fifty stanzas the harmonies show no exhaustion. The theme still inspires, and the variations never become trite or mechanic. It is, as Dr. Schaff has said, "the sweetest and most evangelical hymn of the Middle Ages." We may take any verse at random, and we shall find in it felicities of phrase, tender, plaintive, or joyous, but never phrases only. A pulse beats in every stanza; there is life and love in every line. As, for example:

JESU, DULCIS MEMORIA.

"Quando cor nostrum visitas,
Tunc luce ei veritas,
Mundi vilescit vanitas
Et intus fervet charitas.

"Jesus amor dulcissimus
Et verè suavissimus
Plus millies gratissimus
Quàm dicere sufficimus.

"Qui te gustant, esuriunt ;
Qui bibunt, adhuc sitiunt ;
Desiderare nesciunt,
Nisi Jesum quem cupiunt."

As translated by Caswall :

"When once Thou visitest the heart,
Then truth begins to shine :
Then earthly vanities depart ;
Then wakens love divine.

"Jesu ! Thy mercies are untold,
Through each returning day ;
Thy love exceeds a thousand fold
Whatever we can say.

"Celestial sweetness unalloy'd ;
Who eat Thee hunger still :
Who drink of Thee yet feel a void
Which naught but Thou can fill."

Caswall's translation of the entire hymn is a contribution to English hymnody of unique beauty and worth. Edward Caswall was one of the Oxford clergy whom Newman drew after him to the Church of Rome. Ordained deacon in 1838, and priest the following year, he resigned his incumbency in 1846, and in 1847 was received by Cardinal Acton into the Church, whither his brother and many of his friends had preceded him. Soon after the death of his wife in 1849, Mr. Caswall was reordained, and joined Dr. Newman, at the Oratory, Edgbaston, where he died in 1878. He will be principally remembered, and gratefully remembered, for his translation of Latin hymns, including the whole of those in the Roman Breviary. He wrote a considerable number of original poems, refined, devout, and scholarly, showing, if I am not mistaken, the influence both of Wordsworth and of Keble, but not sufficing to give him a front place among the minor poets of the century. But as a translator of Latin hymns he is surpassed by none, only equalled, perhaps, by Dr. Neale. His renderings are wonderfully close and accurate, his style is pure, and his sense of rhythm gives to his hymns the qualities which have made them so widely popular, pleasant to sing, and easy to remember. Among the best known of them are :

> " Earth has many a noble city."
> " My God, I love Thee ; not because,"
> "Glory be to Jesus."

Many are unsuited to Protestant worship, but all are worthy the attention of the student of Latin hymnology, by whom alone their merits can be fully appreciated.

As Caswall's translation of Bernard's hymn is not generally known beyond the verses found in our hymn books, it will, I think, give pleasure to some to make further acquaintance with it. Here, then, are a few verses taken from the latter part of the hymn :

> " Now have I gain'd my long desire,
> Now what I sought is mine ;
> Now is my heart, O Christ, on fire
> With Thy pure love divine.

> " Blest fire ! which no extinction knows,
> Which never flags or fails ;
> But greater still and greater grows,
> And more and more prevails !

"Blest love! which flows eternally,
  With wondrous sweetness fraught;
Which tasteth most delightfully
  Beyond the reach of thought.

"O joy! O ecstasy of bliss!
  More felt than understood!
What pleasure can compare with this,
  To love the Son of God?

"Come, O Thou King of boundless might!
  Come, majesty ador'd!
Come, and illume me with Thy light,
  My long-expected Lord?

"O fairest of the sons of day!
  More fragrant than the rose,
O brighter than the dazzling ray
  That in the sunbeam glows.

"O Thou whose love alone is all
  That mortal can desire;
Whose image does my heart enthrall,
  And with delight inspire.

"Jesu, my only joy be Thou,
  As Thou my prize wilt be;
Jesu, be Thou my glory now,
  My hope, my victory."

To give a complete account of the various English versions of this hymn would far exceed our limits. By direct translation and by free rendering of selected stanzas, it has furnished more hymns to our modern hymn books than any other production of the Latin Church, a testimony to its evangelical purity and beauty that cannot be mistaken. Much interesting information on this subject will be found in the *Dictionary of Hymnology*. It is a pleasant task to compare the different versions in existence, and to observe with what variety of felicitous phrasing the original is reproduced. Here are different renderings of two stanzas, of which Caswall's translations will be in every reader's memory:

> "Jesu! the hope of souls forlorn!
> How good to them for sin that mourn!
> To them that seek Thee, oh how kind!
> But what art Thou to them that find?
> No tongue of mortal can express,
> No letters write its blessedness;
> Alone who hath Thee in his heart
> Knows, love of Jesus! what Thou art."
> —*J. M. Neale.*

> "Jesu, of penitents the stay,
>   To all that ask how passing kind!
> How good to them that seek the way,
>   But what, oh what, to them that find!
> No tongue can tell, nor heart conceive,
>   Nor pen of readiest writer prove,
> Experience only can believe,
>   What 'tis to live in Jesus' love."
> —*W. J. Copeland.*

> "Jesu, sole hope of contrite heart,
> To those who seek how kind Thou art!
> How good to those that seek Thy face!
> But what to those who find Thy grace?
> No tongue is able to express,
> No pen can write the blessedness;
> But he who will believe may prove
> What raptures spring from Jesu's love."
> —*T. G. Crippen.*

From the free rendering of Dr. Ray Palmer we take a single stanza:

> "Thy truth unchanged hath ever stood;
> Thou savest those that on Thee call;
> To them that seek Thee, Thou art good,
> To them that find Thee, All in all."

But these quotations must end. They are enough to show how the note struck by Bernard long centuries ago has vibrated and does vibrate still in Christian hearts. The great monk's *Joyful Song on the Name of Jesus* "was not for an age, but for all time." Its echoes will continue to be heard wherever that Name is held dear.

CHAPTER VIII.

Hic Breve Vivitur.

(Brief Life is here our portion.)

HYMN 943 in the Wesleyan Hymn Book is divided into four parts, and consists of fifteen eight-line stanzas translated by Dr. Neale from the notable poem of Bernard of Cluny. The author must not be confounded with his great namesake and contemporary St. Bernard, distinguished as Bernard of Clairvaux. The latter, as we have seen, was a great and commanding personage, moving amongst popes and princes—a superior rather than an equal. Throughout his whole career he is conspicuous, a foremost actor in the European drama of his time, and history throws abundant light upon his actions and influence. He died in the year 1153.

The case is wholly different with Bernard of Cluny. Born at Morlaix, in Brittany, and, it is believed, of English parents, he entered the Abbey of Cluny, then ruled by its illustrious Abbot, Peter the Venerable. There he appears to have lived and died, leaving behind him a shadowy name, and the remarkable poem from which our hymn is taken. No other trace of him remains, this great work alone preserving his memory from oblivion.

The monastery of Cluny was one of the most renowned in the whole history of monasticism. Founded as early as the year 912, it attained during the next two centuries a kind of primacy amongst similar institutions, and when at the height of its power and influence some two thousand monasteries, great and small, scattered throughout Europe, conformed to its rule, and looked to Cluny for guidance and direction. At the time when Bernard became a monk of Cluny the great monastery was in all its glory. Its buildings were unsurpassed by any in France, and its services distinguished for their magnificence of ritual. The severity of earlier days had given place to splendour and luxury, and the inevitable process of decay had begun, though as yet not openly or obviously.

Here it was, and amid these conditions, that Bernard composed his memorable poem, *De Contemptu Mundi*, extending to three books, and containing altogether about three thousand lines. The portions printed by Archbishop Trench in his *Sacred Latin Poetry*, and those selected for translation by Dr. Neale, would hardly suggest to a reader the real scope and character of the poem. It is a lamentation over the evil of the times, a satire upon the *immundus mundus*—the foul world in which he lived. The voices of oppression, of misery, of despair reached his ear through the thick convent walls. Around the stately church where he worshipped, around the precincts where he passed his tranquil life, there lay a disordered and distressful world. Even at that great centre of ecclesiastical life pride, worldliness, and corruption were manifest to one who had eyes to see and a heart to feel and to fear. It seemed to him that the end of all things must surely be at hand; that this forgetfulness of God must be the prelude to His coming in judgment. And so his poem begins abruptly with a sternness that startles—

" Hora novissima, tempora pessima sunt, vigilemus.
Ecce minaciter imminet arbiter ille supremus ;
Imminet, imminet, ut mala terminet, æqua coronet ;
Recta remuneret, anxia liberet, æthera donet."

"The world is very evil;
    The times are waxing late;
Be sober and keep vigil,
    The Judge is at the gate.

"The Judge that comes in mercy,
    The Judge that comes in might,
To terminate the evil,
    To diadem the right."

Hora Novissima—"It is the last hour"; the words of the Apostle John (1 Ep. ii. 18) in the Vulgate, "*Filioli, novissima hora est.*" This, without prelude, is the cry with which the poet-monk arrests the ear of the wicked, of the careless, of the devout. "It is the last hour." The Judge is at the door—*minaciter*, bringing vengeance; *imminet, imminet, imminet*—at the door, at the door; it is a trumpet voice uplifted to sinners who have forgotten, and to saints in danger of forgetting. Reserving for the moment any criticism of Dr. Neale's translation as a whole, it must be admitted that the startling tone of Bernard's opening lines is hardly reproduced in the smooth and pleasant English version. Two strains alternate through the entire poem—stern, almost fierce, denunciation of an evil world, and ardent longing for the rest and joy of paradise. The former is deeply, painfully interesting, but hardly lends itself to the uses of Christian song, and both Trench and Neale have made their selections from the latter. The result is that the English reader, while put in possession of some of the loveliest hymns on the heavenly country that have ever been written, receives no adequate idea of the gloom that hangs over a large part of Bernard's poem.

De contemptu mundi—on scorn of the world—is a title under which may be gathered much of the anonymous literature of the twelfth and thirteenth centuries, to say nothing of that which may be found under great names. The people groaned under the oppression of their rulers, ecclesiastical and secular. They were the counters sacrificed in the game of their lords and leaders, the nameless, unconsidered multitude whose lot it was to suffer, whoever took the prizes of the strife. The corruption of the Church was more bitterly resented than that of princes and their courts, for the Church professed righteousness, and held out hopes of peace to which the others made no pretence. Hence there are no mediæval satires so savage as those directed against Rome itself, which, as it claimed spiritual supremacy, incurred bitterest reproach and hatred for its failure to do justice and love mercy. Amid the crowds of idle, profligate monks and scholars who hung around the abbeys and monasteries, or wandered from city to city, there were those of a better sort who despised their rulers, and hated the order of things which they were powerless to change. To such it was a relief—a positive joy—to compose, in monkish Latin, songs or metrical homilies in which they lashed the pride, the avarice, the sensuality of the great ones of the earth, from the Pope downwards. These were sung in taverns, told by the roadside, repeated under their breath by monks in cloisters and refectories. Many were rude and coarse enough; some breathe honest indignation, and are not without true pathos.

The subject is capable of ample illustration, and it is not unworthy the attention of students of history and literature. I shall hope to return to it on another occasion. Here is a stanza or two, roughly translated from an anonymous Latin poem on the Last Judgment:

> "One Judge of all will judge the Judges;
> There a Pope's dignity will go for nothing;
> Bishop or Cardinal, it matters not—
> He shall smell the fumes of Gehenna.
>
> "There'll be nothing to pay to keepers of the seal,
> Nothing to chamberlains, nothing to doorkeepers;
> But prelates shall be given to the torturer;
> Their life will be a death unending.
>
> Prelates shall be punished and Cardinals,
> Abbots and monks and black-gowned nuns,
> Ambitious priests, bribe-loving clergy,
> That scrape together all worldly pelf."

Here and there a loftier soul, like Bernard of Cluny, lifts the subject to a higher level, and with a poet-prophet's indignation warns the wicked of every class that the Judge is at the door.

But along with Bernard's loathing of an evil world was a tender and ardent longing for heaven, the homeland of the redeemed. He is unsurpassed among Christian poets in the intensity of desire, in the joyous anticipation with which he dwells on the glories of the heavenly city, and the blessedness of those who shall gather there. Others have prolonged his notes but none have uttered sweeter, tenderer music than the monk of Cluny.

The metrical form employed by Bernard throughout his long poem is one of the most remarkable that was ever attempted, and I will try to give the English reader an idea of the amazing difficulty which it presents.

Here are four lines ("Brief life is here our portion"), in which the metre may be studied:

"Hĭc brĕvĕ vívĭtŭr, hĭc brĕvĕ plángĭtŭr, hĭc brĕvĕ flétŭr;
Nón brĕvĕ vívĕrĕ, nón brĕvĕ plángĕrĕ, rétrĭbŭétŭr.
O rĕtrĭbútĭŏ, stát brĕvĭs àctĭŏ vítă pĕrénnĭs;
O rĕtrĭbútĭŏ, cǽlĭcă mánsĭŏ, stát lŭĕ plènĭs."

If these lines be read aloud, and the syllables thus accented (´) be duly emphasised, the brief syllables will fall into their place, and the metre will at once make itself felt. It will be seen that the lines are couplets of rhyming hexameters, and that every foot, excepting the last, is a dactyl—*Hic brĕvĕ*, etc. This dactylic rhythm is swift-moving and musical, and has often been employed with good effect in English verse, though our aggregation of consonants is not favourable to so swift a measure. Here are two examples:

"Bríghtest and bést of the sóns of the mórning,
Dáwn on our dárkness and lénd us Thine áid."

"Táke her up ténderly, fáshioned so slénderly, yóung and so fáir."

Bernard's final rhymes, it will be observed, are all double rhymes—*fletur*, retribu*etur*, etc.

Now, this metre is difficult enough to maintain by the thousand lines together, but it is only the beginning of difficulties in the scheme of versification that Bernard has adopted. Going back to the lines already quoted, it will be seen that each line has two internal rhymes in addition to the final rhyme. If the lines be written as follows, the internal, or intermediate, rhymes will be apparent to the eye as well as to the ear:

"Hic breve viv*itur*,
Hic breve plang*itur*,
Hic breve *fletur;*
Non breve viv*ere*,
Non breve plang*ere*,
Retribu*etur*."

The rhymes within the body of the line are technically called *leonines*, and where, as in this instance, the rhyme is confined to the last two syllables of the dactyl, it is a *feminine*, or imperfect, leonine as compared, say, with a *masculine* rhyme like *breviter, leviter*, or *plangitur, frangitur*.

This explanation may appear tedious, and I have no wish to prolong it, but it seemed necessary to point out the extraordinary difficulty of the task the writer set himself, and the wonderfully successful manner in which he dealt with it. His fluent dactyls sweep on without halt or failure, and the six rhymes in every couplet keep time with unvarying precision, weaving a mystic tune that strangely charms the ear. It is little wonder that Bernard attributed the successful accomplishment of his task, if not a penance, surely a work of long and painful effort, to the help of the Divine Spirit. "Not arrogantly, but with all humility," he says, "and therefore boldly, do I affirm, *quia nisi Spiritus sapientiæ et intellectus mihi affuisset et affluxisset, tam difficili metro tam longum opus non sustinuissem* —that unless the Spirit of Wisdom and understanding had been with me and abounded, I could never have composed so long a work in so difficult a metre."

I must reserve for the next chapter some further remarks on the contents of the poem, and on the English hymns derived from it, but as I have quoted four well-known lines with which to illustrate the metre employed,

I may give a translation of the same lines by Mr. C. L. Ford, to whose recently-published translation in the original metre I shall hope to call attention :

"Here, life how vanishing ! short is our banishing, brief is our pain ;
There, life undying, the life without sighing, our measureless gain.
Rich satisfaction ! a moment of action, eternal reward !
Strange retribution ! for depth of pollution, a home with the Lord !"

CHAPTER IX.

Hora Novissima *(continued)*.

THE great poem of Bernard of Cluny, *De contemptu Mundi*, of which a brief account has been given, was practically unknown to English readers until, in 1849, Archbishop Trench published a few extracts from it in the first edition of his *Sacred Latin Poetry*. These selections, only ninety-five lines in all, consist exclusively of passages dwelling upon the joys of Paradise, and the compiler gave to them the title *Laus Patriæ Cælestis*, Praise of the Heavenly Fatherland. By omissions and transpositions an effective and beautiful fragment is presented, but the order is not Bernard's, and the whole is little more than a specimen of one element or strain in the original. But it is the most touching strain in Bernard's poem, the element to which the

Christian heart most readily and deeply responds.

Dr. Trench's selection, beginning "*Hic breve vivitur*," etc., was almost immediately translated by Dr. Neale. Subsequently, however, the latter made a much larger selection of his own, and in 1858 he published *The Rhythm of Bernard de Morlaix, Monk of Cluny, on the Celestial Country*, which contains 218 lines of the original. From this translation is taken Hymn 943 in the Wesleyan Hymn Book, whose parts begin respectively :

> "Brief life is here our portion."
> "For thee, O dear, dear country."
> "Jerusalem the golden," and
> "Jerusalem exulting."

Of the value and permanence of the contribution thus made to the treasury of English hymns there can be no doubt. Taken as separate hymns, which to all intents they are, they at once gained wide popularity. The translation is free, but happy in the extreme. Leaving the exacting and perilous metre of the original, Dr. Neale adopted a swinging, musical ballad metre which, so to speak, almost sings itself, and, without being vulgar, is well adapted to catch the ear and stir the blood. They are found in all the principal hymn books, and must be reckoned amongst the favourite hymns of our time. If we must choose among them, it is to "Jerusalem the golden" that the palm would be generally assigned. The "Heavenly home-sickness," as it has been well called, here finds expression not to be surpassed in Christian song. It is "home-sickness," not morbid or melancholy, but at once childlike in its simplicity, and manly in its ardour, its elevation, its exulting anticipations of noble joys and glorious companionship. At the close of the section ending:

> "Exult, O dust and ashes!
>   The Lord shall be thy part;
> His only, His for ever,
>   Thou shalt be, and thou art,"

the translator adds the note, "I have no

hesitation in saying that I look on these verses of Bernard as the most lovely, in the same way that the *Dies Iræ* is the most sublime, and the *Stabat Mater* the most pathetic of mediæval poems." Elsewhere he writes, "It would be most unthankful did I not express my gratitude to God for the favour He has given some of the centos made from the poem, but especially 'Jerusalem the golden.' It has found a place in some twenty hymnals; and for the last two years it has hardly been possible to read any newspaper which gives prominence to ecclesiastical news without seeing its employment chronicled at some dedication or other festival. It is also a great favourite with Dissenters, and has obtained admission in Roman Catholic services. 'And I say this,' to quote Bernard's own preface, 'in no wise arrogantly, but with all humility, and therefore boldly.' But more thankful still am I that the Cluniac's verses should have soothed the dying hours of many of God's servants: the most striking instance of which I know is related in the memoir published by Mr. Brownlow under the title, 'A little child shall lead them,' where he says that the child of whom he writes, when suffering agonies which the medical attendants declared to be almost unparalleled, would lie without a murmur or motion while the whole 400 lines were read to him."

To this may be added Trench's testimony: " A new hymn which has won such a place in the affections of Christian people as has " Jerusalem the golden " is so priceless an acquisition that I must needs rejoice to have been the first to recall from oblivion the poem that yielded it." This translation is, indeed, Dr. Neale's true monument. A saintly man, an admirable scholar, a poet of real merit, and a learned writer on Church history, ritual, and hymnody, both Latin and Greek, his translations of mediæval hymns constitute his crowning claim to grateful remembrance. In the group of scholars who, under the impulse of the Oxford Movement, set themselves to give new life to the old hymns of the Church by translating them into English, Dr. Neale stands conspicuous. I should be inclined to say—not forgetting the claims of Newman and Caswall—that he is head and chief of them all. Not so cold and reserved as Newman, at once robuster and more versatile than Caswall, Neale had almost every qualification for the work he loved so well—profound acquaintance with mediæval hymnody and the later Latin, ease and vigour of English style, and full command of metre and rhythm. All his translations will be prized by students, but his version of Bernard's hymn has given "a new song" to multitudes. In "Brief life is here our portion," and "Jerusalem the golden," John Mason Neale has built his own monument, and, modest man that he was, secured his memory from oblivion.

In a poem written "in dear memory of John Keble," Neale lovingly recites the great masters of Church song who now received Keble into their company. Ambrose and Prudentius, the two Bernards, Notker, and, best loved of all, Adam of St. Victor—a goodly fellowship in which Neale himself has henceforth a name and a place.

Ambrose.	"He first who twined the mystic notes of Synagogue and Church in one:
Prudentius.	And he, whose thrilling music floats Adown the *Peristephanôn*.
Notker.	"And He who watched from Alpine height The samphire gatherer, and, with breath Bated in terror, learnt to write— 'In midst of life we are in death.'
B. of Clairvaux.	"And Bernard, minstrel of the cross;
B. of Cluny.	And Bernard, who with home sick view, Counting all other joys but loss, Jerusalem the golden drew.
Adam of St. Victor.	"There Adam stands, my Master dear, My dear and reverend Master, first."

There is an attractiveness about the personality of Dr. Neale which those who are very far removed from the men of the Oxford Movement cannot but feel and acknowledge.

As the majority of those who will read these notes are not, perhaps, familiar with Neale's translation, except so far as it is found in our hymn books, I may venture to quote a few additional stanzas:

"And when the Sole Begotten
　　Shall render up once more
The kingdom to the Father,
　　Whose own it was before,

"Then glory yet unheard of
　　Shall shed abroad its ray,
Resolving all enigmas,
　　An endless Sabbath day.

"Then, then from his oppressors
　　The Hebrew shall go free,
And celebrate in triumph
　　The year of Jubilee;

"And the sunlit Land that recks not
　　Of tempest nor of fight
Shall fold within its bosom
　　Each happy Israelite;

"The Home of fadeless splendour,
　　Of flowers that fear no thorn,
Where they shall dwell as children
　　Who here as exiles mourn.

"'Midst power that knows no limit
　　And wisdom free from bound,
The Beatific Vision
　　Shall glad the Saints around;

"The peace of all the faithful,
　　The calm of all the blest,
Inviolate, unvaried,
　　Divinest, sweetest, best."

Neale's version of Bernard's hymn is the only one in popular use, and it is hardly likely that any will be forthcoming to dispossess it, or even to share the place it occupies. There are, however, a few translations that call for attention by reason of the scholarship and the skill shown in reproducing or imitating the original. This intractable metre has challenged and defeated many a translator, and the most skilful have been glad to content themselves with brief encounters and but moderate success. Dr. Neale avoided the contest, chose his own ground, and succeeded on lines of his own. But a few others have aimed at literalness of rendering both of matter and metre.

Mr. Duffield, the American hymnologist, more than thirty years ago produced a version which, judging from the selection I have seen, deserves high praise. Here is a specimen:

> "Pax ibi florida, pascua vivida, viva medulla,
> Nulla molestia, nulla tragœdia, lacryma nulla.
> O sacra potio, sacra refectio, pax animarum
> O pius, O bonus, O placidus sonus, hymnus earum."

> "Peace is there flourishing,
> Pasture land nourishing,
>   Fruitful for ever.
> There is no aching breast,
> There is no breaking rest,
>   Tears are seen never.

> "O sacred draught of bliss!
> Peace like a waft of bliss!
>   Sustenance holy!
> O dear and best of sounds,
> Heard in the rest of sounds,
>   Hymned by the lowly."

The translation by Moultrie, another Oxford scholar and poet, published in 1865 in the *Lyra Mystica*, is better known in this country. It received high praise from Trench, who says: "It very nearly reproduces, and with a success which no one could have ventured to anticipate, the metre of the original."

It is, indeed, a most skilful and felicitous piece of work, perhaps as good as, under the conditions, is possible. Take, for example, his rendering of *Urbs Syon Aurea*, "Jerusalem the golden":

"O Syon bright with gold, flowing with milk thy fold, City
 of Gladness,
Tongue cannot tell thy bliss, heart sinks opprest with this,
 even to sadness.
I cannot strain my sight to that intense delight, nor tell
 the story.
What throbs of ardent love thrill through the courts above,
 how vast their glory!
For Sion's halls along echoes the voice of song: there the
 departed,
Fresh from the deadly fight, throng round the Lord of
 Light, jubilant-hearted.
There is eternal rest; there, after toil, the blest cease from
 life's fever:
There, in heaven's banquet-hall, sound the high festival
 of the Receiver;
There, round the Lord of Might, vested in garments white,
 on that bright morrow
Musters their vast array; tears have all fled away—
 vanished all sorrow."

This is much more skilful work than a casual reader would suppose, but it is safe to say that, as a hymn to be sung, it cannot compete for a moment with the familiar "Jerusalem the golden." Within the last few months, another scholarly hymnologist, Mr. C. L. Ford, has attempted the task, which its very difficulties make attractive, and has published an extremely interesting version, in which the text is arranged in sections and the Latin and the English appear side by side. The original metre is adopted, with the substitution of the single for the double rhyme at the end of the line. English dactyls inevitably become stiff and heavy. They are so consonant-laden that they cannot move as swiftly or trip as lightly as do Latin dactyls; but Mr. Ford succeeds in at least suggesting the original measure and movement. It is, of course, only by making large allowance that we can find five dactyls in such a line as this:

"Christ's Cross doth lighten thee; dark death doth brighten thee, death of thy King."

But in spite of the weight of words under-vowelled or over-consonanted, if the first syllable be sympathetically emphasised the dactylic rhythm will make itself felt. A few lines will suffice to show this. The translation is not literal—it cannot be; but there are many felicities of rendering, and the spirit of the original is well reproduced:

"Loud ring thy portals with songs of immortals, thou martyr's demesne!
Bright with thy denizens, strong in Christ's benisons, lustrous, serene!
Corn for the lowly, and wine for the holy, in thee are increased;
There the King's throne, and the jubilant tone of the march and the feast.
White in arraying, Christ's beauty displaying, the glorified throng
Dwell without weeping in Sion's fair keeping, those palaces strong;
Past all accusing, at rest from confusing of strife or of stain,
Israel by grace is in heaven's high places uplifted to reign.
Peace there doth flourish; green pasture doth nourish with marrow of joy;
Tear never falleth, no terror appalleth, nor foe may annoy.
Holy regaling, the cure for heart's ailing, elixir how blest!
Calm is their singing, that antiphon ringing, that musical rest."

The last line but one would bear revision. The verse is out of step.

We take leave of Bernard. The song beaten out in his cell at Cluny, with much labour and many prayers, is dear to our English homes and churches. Farewell, dear monk and pious soul!

CHAPTER X.

Veni, Veni, Emmanuel.

(O come, O come, Emmanuel.)

THE author of this hymn is unknown. Dr. Neale, its translator, ascribes it to the twelfth century. It is founded on the Antiphons formerly sung in the English Church, and still in the Roman, at Vespers in Advent. The series consists of seven short prayers, mostly in the words of Scripture, and addressed to our Lord under various prophetic designations. They were known as the "Great O's," from the fact that each prayer thus begins, and their use is still indicated in the Calendar of the Prayer Book, December 16, by the words "O sapientia." Their opening words are these:

1. O sapientia, quæ ex ore Altissimi.
2. O Adonai, et dux domus Israel.
3. O Radix Jesse, qui stas in signum.
4. O clavis David, et sceptrum domus.
5. O Oriens, splendor lucis æternæ.
6. O Rex gentium, et desideratus.
7. O Emmanuel, rex et legifer.

The language of which these prayers are composed is that of the Vulgate skilfully interwoven together from the Psalms, the Prophets, and the Apocrypha. Of these the writer of the hymn omitted the first (*O sapientia*), and the sixth (*O Rex gentium*). A prose translation of the remainder, in the order adopted by him, will show what the poet had to work upon, and how successfully both he and his translator wrought in the production, first of the Latin, and then of the English hymn :

1. "O Emmanuel, our King and our Lawgiver. Expectation of the Gentiles, and the Desire thereof; come and save us, O Lord our God."

The poet substitutes Israel for the Gentiles —captive Israel :

> "Veni, veni, Emmanuel!
> Captivum solve Israel!
> Qui gemit in exilio,
> Privatus Dei Filio,
> Gaude! Gaude! Emmanuel
> Nascetur pro te, Israel!"

Nothing can be better than Dr. Neale's rendering :

> "O come, O come, Emmanuel,
> And ransom captive Israel,
> That mourns in lonely exile here
> Until the Son of God appear.
> Rejoice! Rejoice! Emmanuel
> Shall come to thee, O Israel."

Two slight alterations, however, are due to the compilers of *Hymns Ancient and Modern*. They have changed "Draw nigh, draw nigh,' of the translator into "O come, O come"; and in the last line of the refrain they substitute "shall come" for Dr. Neale's more literal, but less euphonious, "shall be born."

2. "O Root of Jesse, which standest for an ensign of the people, at whom the kings shall shut their mouths, unto whom the Gentiles shall seek, come to deliver us, make no tarrying."

The hymn deals very freely with this. It addresses the Rod of Jesse, the "rod and staff" that defend and "comfort" the flock.

> "Veni, O Jesse virgula!
> Ex hostis tuos ungulâ,
> De specu tuos Tartari
> Educet antro barathri."

This is excellently translated :

> "O come, Thou Rod of Jesse, free
> Thine own from Satan's tyranny ;
> From depths of hell Thy people save,
> And give them victory o'er the grave.
> Rejoice !" etc.

Here, also, the compilers have somewhat smoothed Neale's lines.

3. "O Day-spring, brightness of the everlasting light, Sun of Righteousness, come to give light to them that sit in darkness and the shadow of death."

This becomes :

> "Veni, Veni, O Oriens!
> Solare nos adveniens,
> Noctis depelle nebulas,
> Dirasque noctis tenebras.
> Gaude !" etc.

The poet passes by the great titles, *Splendor lucis æternæ*, and *Sol Justitiæ*, but admirably paraphrases the prayer.

Admirable also is the English version :

> "O come, Thou Day-spring, come and cheer
> Our spirits by Thine advent here ;
> Disperse the gloomy clouds of night,
> And death's dark shadows put to flight.
> Rejoice !" etc.

VENI, VENI, EMMANUEL.

I would commend this verse to any student who may read these notes as a well nigh perfect example of accurate and felicitous translation. What is there in the English that was not first in the Latin? What is there in the Latin that is not reproduced in the English?

4. "O Key of David, and Sceptre of the house of Israel; that openest and no man shutteth, and shuttest and no man openeth; come and deliver him that is bound from the prison-house, and him that sitteth in darkness and the shadow of death."

This is abridged in the metrical version:

> "Veni, Clavis Davidica!
> Regna reclude cœlica,
> Fac iter tutum superum
> Et claude vias inferum.
> Gaude!" etc.

Dr. Neale's translation is, again, as close and happy as can be:

> "O come, Thou Key of David, come,
> And open wide our heavenly home:
> Make safe the way that leads on high
> And close the path to misery.
> Rejoice!" etc.

5. "O Adonai, the Ruler of the house of Israel, who didst appear unto Moses in the burning bush, and gavest him the law in Sinai; come to redeem us with outstretched arm."

This is but poorly represented in the hymn, where the last and crowning petition is omitted:

> "Veni, veni, Adonai!
> Qui populo in Sinai
> Legem dedisti vertice
> In majestate gloriæ."

Dr. Neale follows, of course, the metrical version, and does not go to the prose that lies behind it, so that his verse has no reference to the "outstretched arm" by which redemption comes.

> "O come, O come, Thou Lord of might!
> Who to Thy tribes, on Sinai's height,
> In ancient times didst give the law,
> In cloud, and majesty, and awe.
>   Rejoice! Rejoice! Emmanuel
>   Shall come to thee, O Israel."

We are indebted to Dr. Neale for much, as I have previously pointed out; by this hymn he has added to his claims upon our gratitude. It is a *strong* hymn, and one of a class not too largely represented in the Wesleyan Hymn-Book, which is undoubtedly enriched by its presence.

I am only acquainted with one other translation of the *Veni, Veni, Emmanuel.* It is by Dr. Hamilton Macgill, and is found in his *Songs of the Christian Creed and Life,* together with the original, and also in the *Presbyterian Hymnal.* It does not reach the high level of Dr. Neale's version, but has merits of its own.

> "O come! Emmanuel, hear our call!
> And free Thine Israel from her thrall;
> She groans in exile, far from Thee,
> And longs the Son of God to see.
>   Rejoice, O Israel! Wherefore mourn?
>   Emmanuel comes, thy Brother born.
>
> "O come! Thou Rod of Jesse, come!
> Lead Thy down-trodden pilgrims home;
> From hoof of ruthless foe them save,
> From doleful pit, and dreary grave.
>   Rejoice, O Israel! Wherefore mourn?
>   Emmanuel comes, thy Brother born.

VENI, VENI, EMMANUEL.

"O come! Thou Dawn of holier day!
And glad us by Thy heavenly ray;
Our dark clouds scatter by Thy light,
Disperse the shades of death and night.
    Rejoice, O Israel! Wherefore mourn?
    Emmanuel comes, thy Brother born.

"O come, throw wide the gates of heaven;
Thou, to whom David's key is given,
Make safe a pathway from below,
And close the way that leads to woe.
    Rejoice, O Israel! Wherefore mourn?
    Emmanuel comes, thy Brother born.

"O come! O come! Thou Lord of lords,
Whose law, with trump and voice of words,
From Sinai's awful brow was given,
Thy glory filling earth and heaven.
    Rejoice, O Israel! Wherefore mourn?
    Emmanuel comes, thy Brother born."

CHAPTER XI.

Supreme Quales Arbiter.

(Disposer Supreme, and Judge of the Earth.)

THIS is the only Latin hymn in the Wesleyan Hymn Book that is neither ancient nor mediæval. Its author, Jean Baptiste de Santeuil (Santolius Victorinus), a Frenchman, was born in 1630, and died in 1697. Santeuil is a strange companion for Ambrose and Bernard, divided from them by long, momentous centuries, and by differences of character and spirit more important still. The spiritual ideals of the age of Louis XIV. had little in common either with the age that saw the first beginnings of Latin hymnology, or with that which witnessed its splendid consummation. Primitive austerity was gone, and the mediæval fire burnt out. Bishops and abbés were courtiers who crowded the salons of the Grand Monarque, sharing to the full the worldliness of an essentially worldly period, and altogether at home in the society portrayed in the pages of St. Simon and De Retz. The writing of Latin verses of a light, semi-pagan order was one of the most prized accomplishments of the time amongst men who lived in polite society, and the De Santeuil family appears to have possessed the faculty to a high degree, no less than three of the brothers attaining distinction in the art, Jean Baptiste most of all. He was a canon of the monastery of St. Victor, in Paris, the home, five hundred years earlier, of Adam of St. Victor, the most skilful, if not the very greatest, of all Latin hymn-writers. But his vocation did not press heavily upon him. He was a wit, a *bon vivant*, a man of the world well known for his nimble tongue and facile pen. He wrote inscriptions, satires, and society verses full of gods and goddesses, according to the fashion of the day, flattered the King, and bandied jests with his friends, and all this with ease and elegance and an admirable command both of French and Latin. I find among his earlier poems one entitled "The Soap-bubble," and another in praise of the wine of Burgundy. But it is needless to explore any further the singular biography published anonymously three years after his death, with its concluding epitaph :

> "*Cy gît le célèbre Santeüil,
> Poëtes et foux prenez le deuil.*"

> "Here lies renowned Santeüil,
> Poets and madmen, go into mourning."

Here is, indeed, a Saul among the prophets! How came he to be a writer of hymns, and amongst them of one which, in various versions, is found in many of our English hymn books, and in the Wesleyan Hymn Book in particular?

At a certain stage in his career De Santeuil underwent what by an accommodation of the term has been called a "conversion," not a very edifying one, but a change in his literary aims and occupations. The way in which this was brought about is described by his biographer in a paragraph which, for the insight it gives into the spirit of the times, is as good as a whole chapter :

"The late Monsieur Fontanier de Pelisson, who knew him well, urged him to give up mythology and devote himself to Christian subjects, *which would secure him every advantage he could wish.* M. de Santeuil, remembering that his brother had said the very same thing to him before, determined to take the advice, and in future to work only for the Church. In short he wrote to M. de Pelisson his determination on the matter. The King, on account of the honour he had already received from his poems, gave him a State pension of 800 *livres*, which shows the piety of this great monarch, so that, what with the allowance which his family made him, and the presents he received from time to time from the Prince of Condé, etc., he was in possession of a very respectable income."

I must not allow myself to be drawn beyond the limited scope of these papers, or it might be worth while to give some extracts from the poetical epistle in which De Santeuil announces to his friend his intention to write no more profane poetry, and give himself henceforth to pious verse. His biographer gives a French version of the original Latin epistle, which, he says, was lost. In this, however, he was mistaken. It now lies before me as a prologue to the second edition of De Santeuil's *Hymni Sacri*, published in Paris in 1698, the year after his death. It is a wholly artificial composition without a single note of sincerity or deep feeling, in striking contrast, for example, with the lines in which Prudentius turns from pagan literature to consecrate his poetry to Christ and His service. Before leaving this subject it may be said that De Santeuil afterwards forgot his promise, and broke out in verse of a characteristically worldly kind, for which he was severely taken to task by Bossuet, to whom he made an abject apology. De Santeuil was not a bad man, as men went in his time, and among the class to which he belonged, but it is impossible to attribute to him any depth of conviction or reality of religious feeling.

In becoming a religious poet De Santeuil at once found employment for his gifts in connection with the revision of the Paris Breviary, which had just been taken in hand. The Gallican Church at that time preserved a certain independence of Rome, and successfully resisted the Papal endeavour to bring all the Churches to unity of service and ritual. The national feeling which refused to use the Roman Breviary lasted to the beginning of the present century, and in 1670 it led to a scheme for the revision of the Paris Breviary which, in its final form, was issued in 1736, and is known as the Breviary of the Archbishop of Vintimille. A modern French writer on liturgies complains of its anti-papal tone, giving as an illustration the fact that in the service for the Feast of St. Peter the sentence, "Thou art the Shepherd of the sheep, O Prince of the Apostles," is replaced by, "The Lord is Head of the body, the Church; Come, let us adore Him!" De Santeuil's share in the revision of the Breviary was confined to its hymns. It was determined to replace many, if not most, of the old hymns by new ones more in accord with the spirit of the age and the prevailing literary taste. So far as the hymns were concerned this was, I imagine, the chief motive. The simplicity, the quaintness, the rugged metres of an earlier age had become distasteful to the fine gentlemen, lay and clerical, of the age of Louis Quatorze. De Santeuil was the very man to give them a hymnal which would satisfy the taste of the contemporaries of Corneille and Racine, and give them as much, or as little, of Christian doctrine and feeling as they required. He had a scholar's command of language and metre, his style was clear, and characterised by a warmth and brightness which, if they sprang from no depth of conviction, were rhetorically pleasant and effective. There can be no doubt that he threw himself into his task with all the earnestness of which he was capable, and some of his productions suggest that he only just escaped being entirely in earnest.

His hymns at once became popular. At least they enjoyed ecclesiastical and social popularity, which was all that could be looked for in the case of hymns which only the clergy and the gentry could understand. De Santeuil was more than satisfied. They brought him fame and money, and he did not conceal his fondness for either. He would go from church to church to hear them sung. He would recite them with actions and grimaces that amused his hearers—"*avec des contorsions et grimaces à faire peur,*" says his biographer.

I have said that De Santeuil is a strange figure in the goodly fellowship of hymn writers. Still, he is there; and the hymn which has furnished the occasion for these remarks is its own justification for appearing in the Wesleyan Hymn Book. It was written for the Feast of the Apostles, and the main thought is, the treasure in earthen vessels, the power of God made perfect in the weakness of man; and a noble hymn it is, notwithstanding the defects of the writer.

Here are the first four stanzas:

> "Supreme quales Arbiter
> Tibi ministros eligis,
> Tuas opes qui vilibus
> Vasis amas committere!

"Hæc nempe plena lumine
Tu vasa frangi præcipis;
Lux inde magna rumpitur,
Ceu nube scissâ, fulgura.

"Totum per orbem nuntii,
Nubes velut, citi volant;
Verbo graves, Verbo Deo,
Tonant, coruscant, perpluunt.

"Christum sonant: versæ ruunt
Arces superbæ dæmonum;
Circum tubis clangentibus,
Sic versa quondam mœnia."

I may attempt a literal translation:

"What servants dost Thou choose,
O Judge most high,
Who lovest to commit
Thy treasures to mean vessels!

"These vessels filled with flame
Are at Thy bidding broken;
Then a great light bursts forth
As lightnings from a riven cloud.

"Through the whole world Thy messengers
Like clouds fly swiftly forth;
Bearing the Word, the Word Divine,
They thunder, lighten, pour forth rain.

"Their voice says CHRIST! proud citadels
Of demons fall headlong;
As fell those ancient walls
When trumpets clanged around."

The comparison of the apostles to clouds

pouring forth light and rain, may be found in Adam of St. Victor's hymn for the Festival of Saints Peter and Paul, with which De Santeuil, a member of the brotherhood of St. Victor, could not fail to be acquainted.

> "Hi sunt nubes coruscantes
> Terram cordis irrigantes
> Nunc rore nunc pluvia."

> "Clouds they are, light radiating
> Human heart-soil irrigating,
> Now with dew and now with rain."

The *tonant, perpluunt* of the third stanza, "they thunder, they pour forth rain," may also be a reminiscence of a hymn for Pentecost by Adam, in which, speaking of the apostles, he says :

> "Pluunt verbo, tonant minis."

"Their words are rain, their threatenings thunder."

If the reader now examines Hymn 869, he will find it to be a somewhat florid but effective version of the original. As compared with the Latin it shows expansion, but hardly more than is usual in such cases, and the meaning and spirit of the original are well preserved.

The translator is the Rev. Isaac Williams, the friend and pupil of Keble, and a strenuous worker in quiet paths in connection with the Oxford Movement. There is an interesting sketch of his character and career in the *Dictionary of Hymnology*. As now in common use, in *Hymns Ancient and Modern*, the Wesleyan Hymn Book, and others, Dr. Williams's translation has undergone various alterations, as may be seen from the following verse as it first appeared, compared with its present form :

> "They thunder—their sound
> It is Christ the Lord !
> Then Satan doth fear,
> His citadels fall,
> As when the dread trumpets,
> Went forth at Thy word,
> And on the ground lieth
> The Canaanites' wall."

De Santeuil's hymn has also been translated by Chandler:

> "What feeble instruments, O Lord,
> Fulfil Thy wondrous plan ;
> How mean the channels, which convey.
> Thy grace to sinful man."

This is a tame and commonplace rendering. Chambers, in his *Lauda Syon*, gives a more vigorous version, and *The Hymnary* contains one specially written for it by the late C. S. Calverley, so well known by writings, English and Latin, of a very different kind. Here are its two central verses:

> "O'er earth Thy messengers are heard;
>   They haste like clouds before the gale;
> Fraught with the Word, the sacred Word,
>   They pour forth thunder, lightning, hail.
>
> "Christ is their war-cry: at its sound
>   Are hell's proud citadels laid low;
> So, while the trumpets clanged around,
>   Fell once the walls of Jericho."

CHAPTER XII.

Jam Lucis Orto Sidere.

(Once more the sun is beaming bright.)

IN assigning this hymn to Ambrose the compilers of the Hymn Book go beyond what is certainly known. The editors of *Hymns Ancient and Modern* say, more cautiously, "translated from the Latin." It is undoubtedly ancient, and has all the characteristics of the Ambrosian school. In simplicity of theme, in brevity and compactness of utterance, and in its devotional and ethical tone it suggests the "father of Church song" as its author. But evidence of the fact is wanting, and the most careful and learned writers do not include it among the hymns of Ambrose.

We should like to think that it is his, and that so our Hymn Book contains one undoubted hymn by the great Bishop of Milan; for of all the service Ambrose rendered to the

Christian Church, he rendered none more lasting and more fruitful than when he taught his people to find joy and strength in singing hymns, and himself furnished them with songs of prayer and praise. The hymns which drew tears from Augustine in the church at Milan fifteen hundred years ago are still sung, both in their original Latin and in versions of many languages. They served, moreover, as models which many unknown writers followed, until the slender stream of song that flowed from the lips of Ambrose became a river to water and gladden the whole Church of God.

And the stream of Church song was, let it be thankfully recorded, pure at its source, and for some considerable time ran clear and undefiled. In later ages it became turbid and unwholesome enough, but in the hymns of Ambrose and his immediate successors there is no trace of this. Worship was not yet diverted from God to the Virgin and the saints. The "fond inventions" that afterwards darkened Christian doctrine and enfeebled devotion are not found in the Ambrosian hymns. They bear the stamp of simplicity and sincerity. If they lack the emotion, the passionate experience, the self-scrutiny of a later age, they are also free from the ingenuities and sentimentalities which afterwards ran to such lamentable excess. The worshipper contemplates God and not himself. The great objects of the faith are before his soul. He asks for the chief, essential gifts of grace, for "daily bread," rather than for delicate or varied nurture. He has heard the voice of the preacher—"God is in heaven, and thou upon earth; therefore let thy words be few." The strong, terse speech of old Rome, which had seemed to die with a dying paganism, is heard once more in the "new song" of the Church of Christ.

It is to be noted that the themes of these early hymns are chiefly of two kinds. They embody the primary beliefs of the Christian, such as the Advent, the Nativity, the Passion, and the Resurrection of our Lord: or they are designed for use in the morning, the evening, the Lord's Day, or the seasons of the Christian year. The rich developments of modern hymnody may, perhaps, unfit us to recognise at once the merits of these austere and simple utterances. But they have not merely a historic justification in the time and circumstances of their origin; they justify themselves afresh to the devout spirit of every age as uttering greatest truths in fewest words, and expressing in their simplest form the ever-recurring needs of the pilgrim soul.

The hymn before us is a morning hymn:

> "Jam lucis orto sidere
> Deum precemur supplices,
> Nostras ut ipse dirigat
> Lux increata semitas."

> "Once more the sun is beaming bright,
> Once more to God we pray,
> That His eternal light may guide
> And cheer our souls this day."

I have spoken of the "ethical tone" of these hymns. They are largely prayers for grace to live well. "Grant that this day we fall into no sin, neither run into any kind of danger; but that all our doings may be ordered by Thy governance to do always that is righteous in Thy sight," is the prose equivalent or summary of the hymns of this class.

But I must now point out that the translator, the Rev. J. Chandler, has made his English version, not from the original, but from the version in the Paris Breviary, where it appears as altered, lengthened, rewritten in fact, by Charles Coffin. As a writer of hymns Coffin was the successor of Santeuil, of whom I have given some account in a previous chapter, and, like him, contributed largely to the Paris Breviary. Of his original hymns I need not speak. They have their merits, both of sentiment and of style; but it is difficult to understand how he and others should have so cheerfully undertaken to rewrite the most venerable hymns in existence, recasting the work of Ambrose, Hilary, and Gregory, so as to bring it up to the standard of contemporary taste. Coffin's version of "*Jam lucis orto sidere*" presents no point whatever of superiority over the original. It is a little longer and a little tamer, a little less close and strong in texture, and wholly omits the thought with which the original concludes:

> " Ut cum dies abscesserit,
> Noctemque sors reduxerit,
> Mundi per abstinentiam
> Ipsi canamus gloriam."

> " So we, when this new day is gone,
> And night in turn is drawing on,
> With conscience by the world unstained,
> Shall praise His name for victory gained."

This climactic verse disappears from Coffin's version, and consequently has no place in Mr. Chandler's translation. Well might Ambrose, or the unknown author, have anticipated Wesley in saying, " I desire they (the revisers) would not attempt to mend them, for they really are not able. None of them is able to mend either the sense or the verse."

There are English versions of this hymn by Bishop Mant, Dr. Neale, Dr. Newman, Keble, Caswall, Alford, and many others. Some of these, like that in the Wesleyan Hymn Book, are from the Paris Breviary text, but the greater number are from the original. Of

these the most successful is Dr. Neale's well-known
"Now that the daylight fills the sky."

This version is so good that various editors have tried to make it still better; amongst them the compilers of *Hymns Ancient and Modern*, whose arrangement of Neale's translation is so popular as almost to have pushed the original out of sight. I am glad, however, to see that the *Church Hymnary*, henceforth the common hymn book of the Scottish Churches, gives the hymn as it was written. As it is not at present well-known, it may be given here, along with the original. Dr. Neale's translations will well repay a student's attention, though their very excellence is likely enough to discourage him from making any modest attempt of his own.

"Jam lucis orto sidere
Deum precemur supplices,
Ut in diurnis actibus
Nos servet a nocentibus.

"Linguam refrænans temperet,
Ne litis horror insonet;
Visum fovendo contegat,
Ne vanitates hauriat.

JAM LUCIS ORTO SIDERE.

"Sint pura cordis intima ;
Absistat et vecordia :
Carnis terat superbiam,
Potus cibique parcitas :

"Ut cum dies abscesserit,
Noctemque sors reduxerit,
Mundi per abstinentiam,
Ipsi canamus gloriam."

"Now that the daylight fills the sky
We lift our hearts to God on high,
That He, in all we do or say,
Would keep us free from harm to-day—

"Would guard our hearts and tongues from strife,
From anger's din would hide our life,
From all ill sights would turn our eyes,
Would close our ears from vanities.

"Would keep our inmost conscience pure,
Our souls from folly would secure.
Would bid us check the pride of sense
With due and holy abstinence.

"So we, when this new day is gone,
And night in turn is drawing on,
With conscience by the world unstained,
Shall praise His name for victory gained."

CHAPTER XIII.

Angularis Fundamentum Lapis Christus Missus Est.

(Christ is our Corner-stone.)

THE English version of this hymn is by the Rev. John Chandler, one of the earliest of those who, in connection with the Oxford Movement, were drawn to the study of Latin hymnology in the hope of reviving the ancient strain of devotion in the Church. Some translations from the Parisian Breviary, published by the Rev. Isaac Williams, appeared to him to be so "ancient, simple, striking, and devotional" that he was desirous of translating others from the same source, and in 1837 he published a collection of 108 *Hymns of the Primitive Church*. It is characteristic of the period and of the movement referred to that the term "primitive" was applied to anything in the shape of a Latin hymn. The newly kindled enthusiasm had not given itself time to become critical, or Messrs. Williams and Chandler would hardly have gone to the Parisian Breviary for what is ancient or primitive, seeing that the great majority of the hymns which it contains belong to the latter part of the seventeenth century, and those of really primitive origin have lost their ancient character under the hands of revisers.

Mr. Chandler's reference to the originals, which he published along with his translation, is curiously inaccurate and undiscerning. "They bear decided marks of a very remote antiquity. Some may have been very much altered ; some, perhaps, entirely reconstructed, but still as several of them are known to be the work of St. Ambrose and St. Gregory, and other primitive fathers, and if all the rest bear internal evidence of being *about the same age*, they may well deserve the name affixed to them of *The Hymns of the Primitive Church*. That this admirable translator could have taken De Santeuil's Ascension Hymn—

"Nobis Olympo redditus"—

for a hymn of the Primitive Church is amazing. The use of the word "*Olympo*" should have suggested the neo-classical quarter from which it really came.

Dr. J. H. Newman, writing of *The Paris Breviary* in the following year, uses, as might be expected, more guarded language: "Nay, even such (hymns) as the Parisian, which have no equal claims to antiquity, breathe an ancient spirit, and even there they are the work of one pen, are the joint and invisible contribution of many ancient minds."

Both Dr. Williams and Mr. Chandler refer to the unsatisfactory position of the Church of their day—sixty years ago—in respect of hymns for public worship. In spite of a "too numerous list of hymn compilers," and an "immense multitude of rival collections," all lacked sanction and authority. "The fact is," says Mr. Chandler, "there is not, what there surely ought to be in our Establishment, a standard book of Christian hymns, set forth by the spiritual authorities of our Church . . . and it certainly does seem incongruous . . . that we should be left entirely to our own private judgment to provide that whereon so much depends." Each of them cherished the hope that "a proper hymn book would be put forth by proper authority, by the rulers of the Church," a hope which, as all are aware, still remains unfulfilled, and which, we believe, is not now widely cherished, as the want they felt so keenly has been met in other ways, to the general satisfaction of Churchmen. Mr. Chandler offered his translation as a contribution towards the authorised hymn book he desired. Dr. Williams expressed his strong desire that none of his hymns should find unauthorised admission into churches, and, as a matter of fact, they were little suited for congregational use, and there is hardly one among them that has become popular. They possess scholarly and devotional merit, but lack the qualities essential to hymns that people will sing.

Mr. Chandler's translations are freer—less true, perhaps, to the tone of their originals; but they are English hymns of merit, clear in expression, swift-moving and tunable, and many of them have passed into the hymn books in common use.

The Hymn 991 in the Wesleyan Hymn Book is a translation of a part of the fine old hymn—

> "Urbs beata Hierusalem,
> Dicta pacis visio,"

which in the Roman Breviary has been smoothed and flattened almost out of recognition. The Paris version is much nearer to the original, but is weakened by needless alterations.

To show how a hymn can be changed by revision and translation, let the reader compare the same stanzas (1) in the original; (2) in the Roman version; (3) in the Paris version; (4) in an English translation from the Paris version.

Here is the *original*:

> "Angularis fundamentum lapis Christus missus est,
> Qui compage parietum in utroque nectitur,
> Quem Sion sancta suscepit, in quo credens permanet."

The best translation of this I can find is Dr. Neale's:

> "Christ is made the sure Foundation,
> And the precious Corner-stone,
> Who, the two-fold walls surmounting,
> Binds them closely into one;
> Holy Sion's help for ever,
> And her confidence alone."

Here the *crux* for the translator was, how to render the second line. The idea is that Christ, as the Corner-stone, binds together the walls of the city of God, the Jew and the Gentile, of whom it is said, "He hath made both one." This is a fine thought, and quite in the manner of these early hymn-writers, whose acquaintance with the Scriptures was much more close and intimate than is generally supposed. Dr. Neale reproduces the thought, although "the two-fold walls surmounting" is not a very successful rendering of *compage parietum*—by the joining of the walls. This was altered in the *Sarum Hymnal* to

> "Who, the two walls underlying,
> Bound in each, binds both in one."

In the revised Roman Breviary of 1632 the

variations from the original are positively wanton in their sacrifice, not only of archaic phraseology, but of the essential elements of the hymn, substituting other ideas and images for those of the author.

Here is the *Roman* stanza, corresponding to the one given above :

> Alto ex Olympi vertice Summi Parentis Filius,
> Ceu Monte desectus lapis terras in imas decidens,
>   Domus supernæ et infimæ utrumque junxit angulum."

The use of the odious word Olympus, with its suggestion of heathen gods and goddesses, for the Christian heaven shows the taste and feeling of the revisers. The stanza may be rendered thus :

> "From loftiest peak of Heaven (Olympus !)
>   The Son of the Most High Father,
>   Like stone cut from the mountain,
>   Descending to the deeps of earth,
>   Stablishes the corner alike
>   Of His earthly and His heavenly house."

The image of the Foundation Stone is obscured and confused by the reference to Daniel's "stone cut out of the mountain," which is not for building, but to break to pieces, and the mind is sent upon a track that leads away from the true line of thought.

The Paris Breviary differs from the original but very slightly, and faithfully preserves the thought and imagery of the stanza. We may now examine Chandler's translation:

> "Christ is our corner-stone,
>   On Him alone we build;
> With His true saints alone
>   The courts of heaven are filled.
>   On His great love
>   Our hopes we place
>   Of present grace
>   And joys above.
>
> "O then with hymns of praise
>   These hallowed courts shall ring;
> Our voices we will raise
>   The Three in One to sing;
>   And thus proclaim,
>   In joyful song,
>   Both loud and long,
>   That glorious Name.
>
> "Here, gracious God, do Thou
>   For evermore draw nigh;
> Accept each faithful vow,
>   And mark each suppliant sigh;
>   In copious shower
>   On all who pray
>   Each holy day
>   Thy blessing pour.

> "Here may we gain from heaven
> The grace which we implore;
> And may that grace, once given,
> Be with us evermore,
> Until that day
> When all the blest
> To endless rest
> Are called away."

This is an admirable English hymn, worthy of the wide popularity it has attained, and perhaps the translator has done better service by the free treatment of his theme, and by the modern key in which he has set it, than if he had attempted a closer rendering of the original.

It will be observed that the reference in the first verse to the binding together of the walls is wholly omitted, and another, more general, idea is substituted. A close examination of the other verses will show a similar preference for free paraphrase as against strict translation. In spite of his sincere, though not very discriminating, reverence for antiquity, Mr. Chandler was essentially modern in religious sentiment. His translations sit loosely to their originals, and his "primitive" hymns are good

Anglican compositions, disappointing, perhaps, to the student of Latin hymnology, but a valuable addition to sacred song in the modern Church.

Dr. Neale's (revised) translation is much closer to the language and spirit of the original:

> "Christ is made the sure foundation,
>   And the precious corner-stone,
> Who the two walls underlying,
>   Bound in each, binds both in one:
> Holy Zion's help for ever,
>   And her confidence alone.
>
> "All that dedicated city,
>   Dearly loved by God on high,
> In exultant jubilation
>   Pours perpetual melody,
> God the One-in-Three adoring
>   In glad hymns eternally."

It has already been mentioned that this hymn, which has a completeness of its own, is part of a longer hymn beginning, *Urbs beata Hierusalem*. The entire hymn is given in Trench's *Sacred Latin Poetry*. It is known through Dr. Neale's English version:

> "Blessed city, heavenly Salem,
>   Vision dear of peace and love."

Its unknown author touched a chord that is heard again in such hymns as "Jerusalem! my happy home!" "Jerusalem on high my song and city is," and many another song of desire for the rest that remaineth.

> "O happie harbour of the saints!
>   O sweete and pleasant soyle!
> In thee noe sorrow may be found,
>   Noe greefe, noe care, noe toyle.
> There lust and lukar cannot dwell,
>   There envy bears no sway;
> There is no hunger, heate, nor colde,
>   But pleasure everie way.
> Hierusalem! Hierusalem!
>   God grant I soon may see
> Thy endless joyes; and of the same
>   Partaker aye to bee."

CHAPTER XIV.

Dies Iræ, Dies Illa.

THE *Dies Iræ* is, undoubtedly, the supreme hymn in the treasury of the Latin Church, perhaps the greatest in the whole domain of Christian hymnology. For six centuries it has moved the minds of men of various nations and creeds by its overwhelming solemnity and pathos. The explanation of its hold upon the Christian Church is to be found in the theme itself, in the spirit of its treatment, and in its perfection of literary form—language, rhythm, and metre combining with an effect that has never been surpassed.

The subject of the hymn is the most dread of all, alike to the devout and to the careless, The Day of Judgment—"That Day." The first line, by which it is generally known and referred to, is taken from the Vulgate version of the prophet Zephaniah (i. 15):

"Dies iræ, dies illa, dies tribulationis et angustiæ, dies calamitatis et miseriæ . . . dies tubæ et clangoris."

"Day of wrath, that day, day of trouble and distress, of calamity and desolation . . . day of the trumpet and of alarm."

These words, with their deeper echoes in the New Testament, have tolled like a bell in many ears, but they passed into the soul of an obscure monk of the thirteenth century to stir it to its depths and to make him a prophet and a psalmist for all time. He feels the earth tremble at the coming of the Judge. The heavens are ready to flee away. At the sound of the trumpet the dead of all lands gather before the throne. The book is opened for judgment. In stanzas that move slowly, but never pause, the solemn pageant is described as by one that sees it. The vision unfolds before him. He looks until he can look no more. "What shall I say then, wretch that I am, on what helper shall I call, when scarcely shall the righteous be saved?

O King of Glory, Fount of Mercy, save me! Remember, merciful Jesus, it was for me Thou didst come to earth. In search of me Thou wast weary, Thou didst endure the cross. Let not such labour be in vain. . . . Who didst pardon Mary, and hearken to the dying thief, Thou biddest even me to hope. Of no worth are my prayers, yet of Thy goodness show me mercy lest I perish for ever."

Such is the strain, in meagre paraphrase, of this immortal hymn. It is not an uncommon or infrequent one in Christian hymnody, but it has often been embodied in verse which, in spite of the greatness of the theme, we are compelled to call flat and uninspired. Instances may be found in almost any hymn book where the most solemn truths of religion are set forth in metrical form, carefully drawn out stanza by stanza—the intention to edify being obvious from beginning to end; and yet we are not reached. The hymn does not justify itself as a hymn, and so far from receiving additional force or vividness, truth is lowered and enfeebled by the dull and conventional way in which it is presented. The explanation of this is generally twofold: a shallowness and inadequacy both spiritual and intellectual. There are themes that should not be attempted except by strong souls deeply moved. Smooth, level-running natures may suffice for common tasks, but there are visions that they cannot see, voices that they cannot hear, and words which it is not theirs to speak.

We know little of Thomas of Celano, the friend and disciple of Francis of Assisi, save that he wrote the *Dies Iræ*. It is enough. We know all we need to know. To him the Last Judgment was no mere formal article of belief, no vague, indefinite doctrine lying away behind the everyday matters of faith and practice. It had been revealed to him. The awful vision had risen before him. Its nearness made all other things remote; its reality made the heavens and the earth that now are unreal. It was said of Dante, as he moved silently along the street, "He has seen hell"; it might be said of Thomas, "He has seen the great white throne, and Him that sits upon it." This is the first element of power in the *Dies Iræ*. Its writer has seen, has felt. It seems to be a law of the spiritual kingdom that great truths should be revealed first to chosen and prepared souls, and through them should reach the multitude, unfit to be called to the mount of vision and to speak face to face with God. The prophet sees that which other men must see through his eyes; he hears that in secret which others must hear from his lips. How many congregations, through all these centuries, have repeated the confession of belief, " From thence He shall come to judge the quick and the dead," and how faint and far-off has been, for the most part, the apprehension of judgment to come! But now and again it has been given to some soul that could receive it—one, perhaps, or two in a century—to be so penetrated and possessed with the vision of "the last things," that it has been able to break the slumbers of the Church, and send a strong, disquieting voice through the busy world itself. Such a soul was that of Thomas of Celano, and such the mission he accomplished.

The age in which he lived was one that multiplied intercessors, that built up the doctrine of Mary's mediatorial office, and elaborated its systems of penance and satisfaction, of absolution and indulgence. In later ages still, these developments were drawn out to unimaginable length and detail. Hence, in the hymnaries and service-books of the Latin Church the *Dies Iræ* has strange companions. It is surrounded by hymns to the saints, by laudations and invocations addressed to those of whom it may be said, "None of them can by any means redeem his brother, nor give to God a ransom for him." All the more noteworthy is the absence from the *Dies Iræ* of any mention of such. The soul is alone with God. It approaches Him without the intervention of Church or priest. It does not call upon the Queen of Heaven to command or to entreat her Son. No *Mater dolorosa* or *Mater speciosa* intercepts for a moment the gaze that is fastened on the Redeemer. Nor are prayers and penance counted as a price, or part of a price:

> "Preces meæ non sunt dignæ,
> Sed Tu bonus fac benigne,
> Ne perenni cremer igne."
>
> All unworthy is my prayer
> Make my soul Thy mercy's care,
> And from fire eternal spare.
> —(*Alford.*)

Throughout the entire hymn there is no infection of the time, no local taint or blemish to be allowed for, or to be removed, by later, revising hands. If in language and literary form it belongs to the thirteenth century, that is all. In essence and spirit it is neither patristic, nor mediæval, nor modern ; for penitence and humble trust in the mercy of God are the same in all ages. We set the prayer of Thomas of Celano side by side with that of Toplady, the thirteenth century with the eighteenth, the Latin with the English, and "there is no difference."

> "Preces meæ non sunt dignæ."
> "In my hand no price I bring,
> Simply to Thy Cross I cling,"

Concerning the merits of the *Dies Iræ* as a

poem in which language, metre, and rhythm are perfectly combined to produce an overwhelming effect, there is unanimity of judgment. The learned, the critical, the devout, are of one mind, and record one verdict. It has attracted more attention, and has been more frequently translated than any other hymn. It is indissolubly associated with the genius of Goethe and of Mozart, with the tears of Johnson and the deathbed of Walter Scott. Archbishop Trench says of it: "The metre so grandly devised . . . the solemn effect of the triple rhyme, which has been likened to blow following blow of the hammer on the anvil—the confidence of the poet in the universal interest of his theme, a confidence which has made him set out his matter with so majestic and unadorned a plainness as at once to be intelligible to all—these merits, with many more, have given to the *Dies Iræ* a foremost place among the masterpieces of sacred song."

Similar tributes from scholars and hymnologists might be quoted. One only can be given, translated and abridged from the *Thesaurus*

Hymnologicus of Daniel: " By common consent it is the chief glory of sacred poetry and the most precious treasure of the Latin Church. Even those who know nothing of Latin hymns assuredly know this, and they who are unmoved by the sweetness of holy song cannot but give heed to this hymn, whose every word is a thunder tone. Its very theme is such that one must needs give ear. As the strain proceeds we seem to behold Christ sitting upon the throne, and heaven and earth shaken by His dread voice, to hear the sound of the trumpet that opens the graves and awakes the dead, and we ourselves are borne, as it were, through the air, and, smitten by terrors of conscience, along with all mankind implore the mercy of God. Who does not feel what majesty the Latin tongue, whose distinction indeed is majesty, lends to this hymn, how aptly the whole poem is framed, how wonderfully the verses move, like waves of the sea, and what solemnity is born of the triple rhymes in each strophe? For these reasons, as I think, it has come to pass that all Christian people, not merely those of the Church that gave it birth, but of the Reformed Church, hold this hymn in highest honour."

Although there are well nigh innumerable versions of the *Dies Iræ* in English and in German, it is not too much to say that it has not been, and that it cannot be, adequately translated. Those who would know its true grandeur and beauty, its solemnity and sweetness, must read it in its own unalterable, untranslatable Latin. It is, indeed, to use Daniel's expression, *Latinissimus* — essentially and characteristically Latin, not only in diction, but in quality and tone.

Let the reader, with such knowledge of Latin as he may possess, take this great hymn reverently in hand. In the mere construing he will find few difficulties. The language is simple, the construction uninvolved, and the thought pauses at the end of each three-lined stanza. Allusions which could not be found in a classical Latin composition, or be understood by a contemporary of Horace or Cicero, will be intelligible to him, and the special meaning which Christianity has given to words previously used in a lower or more general sense will be recognised at once.

" Quando Judex est venturus."
"Tuba mirum sparget sonum."

The reader knows what *Judge* it is who will come, and what *trumpet* it is that will send its dread sound through the sepulchres of earth.

" Quum resurget creatura."

Here are two words, one of which had its meaning immeasurably deepened in Christian use—for *resurgere* never meant to rise from the dead, until Christ had risen ; and the other is a word formed to express an idea that had no clear existence for the heathen mind.

" Liber scriptus proferetur."

The book that is written will be brought forth. No need to ask *what* book, though all Pagan Rome could not have told. And so throughout the hymn, a reader with but "small Latin" will follow the meaning, though he may not know through what rebirths and baptisms the words had passed before they could carry the meaning which now speaks directly to his understanding and his heart.

But he will do well to linger upon each line, to try its music with his ear, and surrender himself alike to the meditation, the adoration, and the entreaty through which the poem moves, while terror, humility, and impassioned prayer successively mould the language to their use. What is there in human literature more tremendous in thought and in expression than the lines—

> "Tuba mirum spargens sonum
> Per sepulchra regionum,
> Coget omnes ante thronum"?

Or what is there in ancient or modern verse more tender and moving than the prayer—

> "Recordare, Jesu pie,
> Quod sum causa Tuæ viæ;
> Ne me perdas illâ die.
>
> "Quærens me sedisti lassus,
> Redimisti cruce passus;
> Tantus labor non sit cassus"?

In our feebler English perhaps this cannot be better rendered than in the version of Dr. Irons—

> " Think, kind Jesu!—my salvation
> Caused Thy wondrous Incarnation;
> Leave me not to reprobation!

> " Faint and weary Thou hast sought me,
> On the Cross of suffering bought me;
> Shall such grace be vainly brought me?"

But let it be said again, and as a last word, that this oft-translated hymn is untranslatable, and that no version can do more than faintly suggest the qualities which make it unique in the treasury of the Church's song.

www.ingramcontent.com/pod-product-compliance
Lightning Source LLC
Chambersburg PA
CBHW030259170426
43202CB00009B/813